Meeting the Moment

A Spoken Word Poetry Collection

By Evan B. Carr

Tetraktys Press
Lansing, MI

Copyright © 2024 by Evan B. Carr

All rights reserved.

No portion of this book may be reproduced in any form without written permission from the publisher or author, except as permitted by U.S. copyright law.

ISBN: 978-1-966704-01-0

First Edition

Library of Congress Control Number: 2024927417

Art by Evan B. Carr Copyright © 2024
Cover design by Evan B. Carr

Contact
www.evanbcarr.com
evan@evanbcarr.com

To my parents who
gave me the most
precious gift – life.

Thank you.

And to Jessica,
Because
Love.

Table of Contents

I. Muse
- My Muse
- Staring Contest
- Subject? Object?

II. Language
- We Made It All Up
- Precious Time
- Western Mutt

III. Humanity
- The Day Will Come
- Collective Trauma
- Harmonizing Poles

IV. Modernity
- Eight Billion People
- Nightly Walk
- Blue Truck
- Mass Shooting
- dirty bubbles
- What a Time to Be Alive

V. Capital
- Hedge Fucks
- Name Your Price
- More Or Less
- What Really Matters

VI. Interlude
- Squish Factor
- I Used to Beat Dead Horses
- Break Up Surprise
- Fertile Words
- Human Behavior

VII. Healing
- Savory Gun
- S P A C E
- Flawed Reflection
- Neuro
- Manhood
- Conformists Together

VIII. Soul
- The Puzzler
- I Was There
- Developmental Wheel
- The Seed
- The Greatest Investment You'll Ever Make

IX. life : nature
- do you remember rain?
- It Beckons
- Lock Her Up
- River Of Our Own Knowing

This collection is intended to be read chronologically.
Each section builds on the last as a developmental journey.

X. Seasons
- Ode to Fall
- Winter Snow Day
- A Single Drop
- Forest

XI. Place
- Hear, Here!
- Manistee
- Tree Says

XII. Body
- Skin's Memory
- Your Body Will Save You
- Massage
- Taken
-

XIII. Love
- Ten Tears
- New Love Matrix
- All of That
- Flight's Booked

XIV. Surrender
- Surrender
- Illusion of Control
- God's Design

XV. Meeting the Moment
- Not They
- Gordian Knot
- In This Time Sun
- Eco Anxiety

XVI. Hope
- Hope For Democracy
- Problem to Potential
- zero to ONE

XVII. Epilogue

XVIII. About the Author

XIX. Photo Credits

I. Muse

It's hard to know if one writes poetry, or if one is written by the poem itself. From where does poetry emerge? Deep beneath the waking reality of middle-world appearances lives the Muse. Shrouded in Mystery and speaking in the language of symbols, images, and myth, the Muse whispers inspiration to those willing to listen.

My Muse

My phone rings instantly I'm excited
Thinking it's you who's calling uninvited
I realize it's not and fear my love's unrequited
Spirit in action yet I feel so shortsighted

Tender days I long for your touch
Another could press my skin the same but it differs much
Your skin is alive with a deep recollection
Of all our cherished history and sweet sweet affection

Soul wrote the script I haven't yet remembered the plot
That somehow this is a gift soil scooped in a pot
Birthing beginnings new roots 'n no rot
Like a spider spinning or a shepherd with her flock

My heart is my guidestone it'll never again waiver
Risking it all not afraid of a crater
Or a divet rivet give it a ding or a nick
Life's admission heart's truth ya don't gotta think quick

Find peace not away but by moving right through
All that I resist 'n don't wanna go into
Peel layer after layer until I find the truth
No matter how deep I dig all I keep finding is you

Night sky's stars remind me of all that is holy
Beyond all the programming trying to control me
Slowly, so slowly our positions progress
Reflections of true colors released with my breath

From the well springs eternal this life and my being
A kernel of truth liberation so freeing
We could never be separate now that I'm seeing
My love in proportion of all that I'm grieving

In the void hangs a moment pregnant with potential
Seeds of life's inspiration deemed quite essential
Passion and grace and all it entails
Require leaps of faith beyond the details

Behind the wind lies a stillness of God's design
A template of perfection polarity entwined
In a tango or waltz beauty donned and enshrined
Through energies entangled and bonded in time

From expansion and action come contraction and pause
Reaction to response and insight into cause
Experience births wisdom and that is because
There are no mistakes despite illusory flaws

The saeculum passes in cyclical fashion
Celestial progression below we are matching
What is written above a guide to our lives
Hermetic correspondence before our very eyes

Gratitude abound every moment a gift
Even in the tempest when floating adrift
Without paddle or rudder we pray for a lift
Words uttered back by God "no thing is amiss"

And yet faith fails these festering doubts
Pestering thoughts that can't be driven out
By struggle, hope, or by wish, a route
To be taken cannot be switched

A river flows as a tree grows in no other way
It's nature enfolded as night is to day
Memories once forgotten unfolded DNA
Emboldened expressions and purpose at play

Wrapped in such beauty embraced and caressed
Vulnerably seen felt and undressed
Held and affirmed resting gently on breast
Giving no other way she's simply the best

Great unknown fog courage penetrated
The sacred veil of fear its illusion generated
Now seen and released by effort or not
Your truths venerated by the lessons you sought

In this hologram it is seen that all is sacred
Infinite possibilities one's for you just be patient
And practice discernment find comfort in waiting
For divine invitations that are yours for the taking

If you ever wish for something more than this moment
Presence begs your attendance to show up and own it
Daydreams beckon lost in how you wrote it
Yet you're dreaming reality to now stay devoted

Never one way two opposites in reverse
As love is to hate pleasure redefines hurt
Choice is temporal the whole spectrum flirts
In subtle gradations of feelings diverse

Her melody flutters teach learning through hymn
Cacophony utters to each a great yearning within
If butterfly morphs from larva to flight in the wind
Then soon you'll see yourself surrounded by kin

Your eminence claimed by right of your birth
Remembrance enflamed by your might and your worth
Many watch expectantly awaiting your hearth
Heart's inheritance fired up in your work

The beauty of time we grow together it unfolds
Majestically telling tales that are ours to be told
The cycles of our trifles and the joys in wrinkles
The stories of old in crow's feet twinkles

Tides won't relent til Spirit of Death beckons
That moment to repent, reflect, and to reckon
Of choices made not long since forgot
No reticence will change what you make as your lot

Now wonder with child's eyes hither and yon
Heart open wide with love as your bond
To all that you see and in how you respond
Unlocking the mysteries of the Great Beyond

Staring Contest

Come to the page no words confused just a blank gaze
Line's empty like amusement parks on rainy days
You're not tall enough to ride so come back later
Flustered, pen's too heavy to scroll 'cross this paper
And even if you could muster the flow
You know, it wouldn't be good enough to show
Or speak aloud, handicapped by these doubts
When you share on social accounts
You'll probably be denounced
As just another voice barely remarkable
Nothing clever or valuable hardly marketable
This internal talk track it's a great giant boulder
A high personal standard such a weight on your shoulders
That the page is still blank it just lies their goading
To your credit, you don't resort to moping
Resolutely staring back vacant as the container
Committed to write who will blink first in the remainder
Of time you've allotted before you sigh in relief
Back again tomorrow, hope it goes better, good grief

Subject? Object?

Do I drum, or does the drum drum me?
Do I write poetry, or does the poetry write me?
Do I do spoken word, or am I word spoken?
Am I the chooser, or am I the chosen?
What is the relationship between the doer and the deed?
Between subject and object, the seer and the seen?
Am I dreaming of life, or is life itself dreamed?
Am I a human doing, more than I'm a human being?
Do I have my fear and trauma, or does fear and trauma have me?
Do I see the forest for the trees, or perhaps I just see trees?
Does it seem I'm about to burst, or am I bursting at the seams?
Am I full of questions, or are the questions full of me?

II. Language

Language is humanity's most important tool.
With it we have created everything. How
quickly we forget that we made it all up…

We Made It All Up

YOU DO KNOW WE MADE IT ALL UP? LIKE OUR CITIES AND UNIVERSITIES, BOOKS, MOVIES, TV, LAWS, POPULAR CULTURE, JOBS, AND **TECHNOLOGY**...NONE OF ITS IN OUR **BIOLOGY** IT WAS IMAGINED ONE DAY BY SOMEONE LIKE AN ARTIST STARTS WITH A BLANK CANVAS AND **FRAME**/ THEY USED THE MOST IMPORTANT **TECHNOLOGY** EVER INVENTED TO GIVE IT A **NAME**: **LANGUAGE**, IT AT ONCE IS THE SUM OF OUR SPECIES' POSSIBILITY AND THE BANE OF OUR EXISTENCE, THE MEDIUM THROUGH WHICH PERSONAL TRIUMPH AND COLLECTIVE CATASTROPHE **OCCUR** / THINK ABOUT IT THIS PIECE ITSELF IS PURE **WORDS** THE SOUNDS BOUNCE AROUND **YOUR BRAIN** UNTIL YOU'RE SURE ITS MEANING, WHAT OCCURS WITHOUT LANGUAGE? OUR MOST POWERFUL TOOL THAT BUILT HAMMURABI'S CODE AND THE FORTUNE 500 / OUR **MOST POWERFUL** WEAPON EMPLOYED SO EFFECTIVELY BY DICTATORS, DESPOTS, AND CULT LEADERS / FOR ALL OUR **ANTICS** - LOVE, HATE, THE FULL SPECTRUM OF **EMOTION** INFORMATION, MEMORIES, FACTS, WAR, **PRANKS**, **SEX**, ALL OUR ACTIONS, WE COMPREHEND BECAUSE WE MAKE **SEMANTIC** MAPS / **THANKS** TO THE **EXPLOSION** OF THE **CORTEX** WE'RE BASICALLY WALKING **DICTIONARIES** WITH A **MOUTH** HAVE YOU EVER STOPPED TO FIGURE **OUT** WHY SOMETHING HAS THE NAME IT DOES AND DOESN'T IT SEEM VERY **ARBITRARY**? LIKE WHY IS A CAR A **CAR**, AND A STEERING WHEEL A STEERING **WHEEL**? WHAT IF A CAR WASN'T A CAR BUT A **GUITAR**? AND A STEERING WHEEL AN **ORANGE PEEL**. DOES THAT MEAN I HOP IN MY GUITAR AND GRIP THE ORANGE PEEL ON MY TRIP TO THE FUTBALL **GAME**? IT WOULDN'T SOUND **STRANGE** TO US BECAUSE WE'D KNOW IT BY NO OTHER **NAME** / HOW MUCH IS ENCODED IN THE LANGUAGE WE THINK AND **SELF-AFFIRM** / AND THE WORDS WE'RE SPEAKING LIKE THE DIFFERENCE BETWEEN A NOUN AND A **VERB** / THE FORMER IS IMPOSSIBLE THE LATTER THE VERY NATURE OF **BEING** / IN SOME LANGUAGES THERE'S NO SUCH THING AS A **NOUN**, NO STATIONARY FIXED OBJECT YOU CAN PUT **DOWN** THERE IS ONLY THE **BECOMING** / THE **SKY IS SKYING**, THE **SUN IS SUNNING**, THE **TREE IS TREEING**, EVERYTHING IS NO-THING BUT AN **EMERGENT STATE OF BEING** AN ENCODING THAT THE MATERIAL WORLD IS TEMPORARY AND **TRANSITORY** MEANING ITSELF IS MADE ONLY OF METAPHORS AND **ALLEGORIES** / MYTHS AND **STORIES** BREWED IN OUR IN OUR **IMAGINATION** UP FOR **INTERPRETATION** AND ONLY VALUABLE WHEN UNDERSTOOD IN **RELATION** / A CHAIR, **THE WORD CHAIR**, IS MEANINGLESS WHEN NOT TAKEN IN **CONTEXT** WITH TABLE, FLOOR, SITTING, TIREDNESS, SUPPORT, **STABILITY, EXCETERA** / WHAT A **PLETHORA** OF **POSSIBILITY** RHYME, METER, INTONATION ON **TONGUE** / VOLUME, CADENCE, INSINUATION'S **SUNG** / LEXICON **LOQUACIOUS** WORD CHOICE FOR THE **NAMELESS** PRECIOUS **VIVACIOUS** LANGUAGE EACH OF US SITS IN A COCKPIT OF **SOARING POTENTIAL** WORDS CAN BE **BORING BLESSINGS** JUST AS MUCH AS **ESSENTIAL WEAPONS** / CHOOSE CAREFULLY AND CREATE ONLY WHATS WORTH **EXPRESSING** / THERE'S ELEGANCE IN **SIMPLICITY** AND **PRECISION** / BREVITY IS THE SOUL OF WIT...RIGHT SPEECH IS YOUR **DECISION**

precious time

ever lurching forward
toward searching for rest
divided indeterminate
every second a test
lodged between the past
and the future as it careens
fast like a big-bang explosion
creating each day from smithereens
the clock of our lives is beholden
to some force that dreams
driving all matter toward erosion
no thing surviving save for the pattern
of each moment after the last
a devotion to linearity
marching with regularity
relentless persistence
existence watches the tale
life is a temptress
her details lost in a veil
of time's unspeakable scale
finally seeing how our tiny lives pale
and that's what makes them
so undeniably
precious

Western Mutt

I'm white a Western European mutt
Proud to be a thirteenth-generation American but
In the melting pot the ancestors' ways were lost
What were their traditions? And what is the cost
Of the lineage of this blood that was forsaken?
This DNA aches to recollect my people's ancient
Ways of relating white washed our inheritance taken.
We need this now more than ever, there's no time to be patient.
You see there's wisdom in the language in the natural tongue
The beauty of describing the world on how songs were sung
The Power of each particular word chosen
How wisdom was passed down generation's truth spoken
The continuity of our oral line's been broken.
Within me I can feel those encodings—they live on
I am that which they were hoping for, I belong
To more than I understand how my feet long
To walk our land, slowly, step by step
As I talk and breathe deeply to reconnect
My heart wells with majesty and deep respect
Tears for the travesties and how little is left.
What is my heritage? And what is my culture?
Have I been imprinted by American vultures?
Have I learned to be a taker and rarely a sharer?
How would you have me be, o wise forebearer?

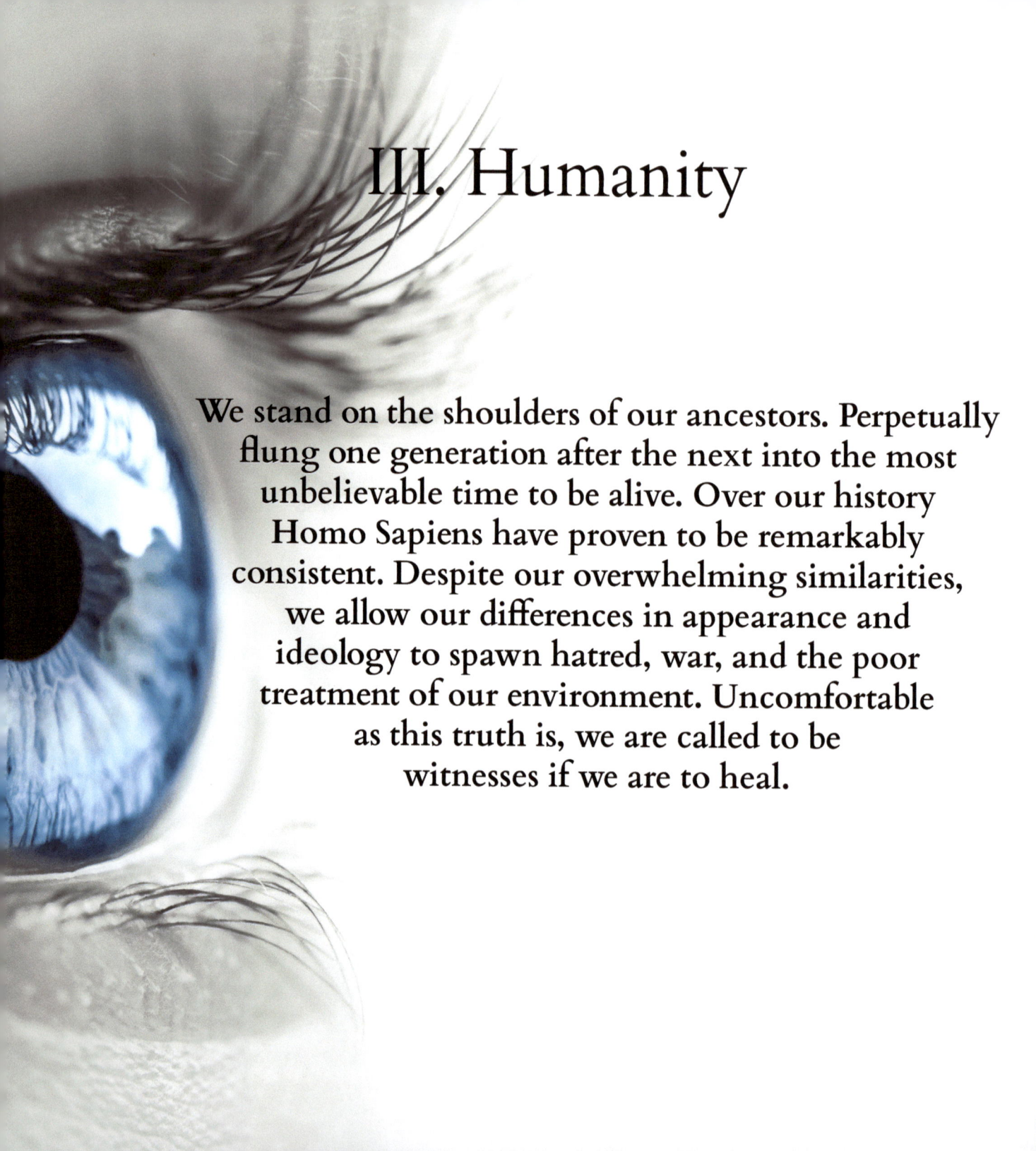

III. Humanity

We stand on the shoulders of our ancestors. Perpetually flung one generation after the next into the most unbelievable time to be alive. Over our history Homo Sapiens have proven to be remarkably consistent. Despite our overwhelming similarities, we allow our differences in appearance and ideology to spawn hatred, war, and the poor treatment of our environment. Uncomfortable as this truth is, we are called to be witnesses if we are to heal.

Soon, the day will come
When you have no choice
But to look out upon the vast
Decimated land from
Which you come.
Smoldering ash
Forests feeening
For parched lake beds of trash
Under particulated
Breathing
And water bodies' found
Seething with sludge
Reality's sealed like a dated
Letter already nudged
Down into the mailbox
Sent an inescapable fate.

Even reliable hindsight
Might need lenses
To see how you sauntered
Without caring to this barren
Stupendous
And scary life-denying result
Sown at the very time of this recount.
When crying
You yet might doubt
Or ponder:
Who's at fault?
Why didn't we act?
When we first grasped
The truth of yore
With all the facts
A useless
Question for
The rest of your
Desperate gasps.

As your eyes burn
Like the devastation
Raging incredulously
Like the forest fires
That no longer burn for a lack of fuel,
How could they have done this to me?
You inquire
As you engage in review
Lamenting your inaction, or
Celebrating your uptake
Both of which
May have been
Too little
Too late
To save the dead
Your tears failing to lubricate
The dry riverbed.

Collective Trauma

Limey, Whitey, and Wop
Wigger, Wetback, and Uzkrop
My God, When will we stop?
Towel head, Snowflake, and Tonto
Slant, Squaw, Slope, and Sambo
It's time to retire these words, Pronto.
Redskin, Chicano, Pajeet, and Kimchi
Paddy, Monkey, Nip, and Gypsy
Derogatory slang, height of hypocrisy.
Kraut, Kike, Jigaboo, and Kemosabe
Jap, Injun, Hike, Hunk, Heeb, and Hymie
Words so unbelievably far past grimy.
Haji, Guido, Greaseball, Goombah, and Gook
Ali Baba, Beaner, Buddhahead, and Coon
Perpetuating hate, may these words die soon.
Frog , Flip, Coconut, and Dink
Apple, Ape, Cracker, and Chink
Each of these words is far worse than you think.
They come encoded with a whole history of hate,
Unless you've been on the receiving side you cannot relate,
Except somewhere up the line most of us had ancestors who dealt with this fate.
If you think these sentiments are a thing of the past you haven't been
paying attention to what's been happening in the United States.
Bigotry and hatred no longer hide in the closet,
Many of us grew up with prejudiced influences if we're honest,
From our parents, friends, or television,
Words like daggers to others make the sharpest attacks.
How do we heal this darkness when so many are attached
To the past and these decimating methods of exclusion?
"They are not worthy," it's thought, "not worthy of inclusion."
As long as the illusion of separation exists,
The confusion over the human race's restoration will persist.
Tribalism has infiltrated minds, it will not go away
Despite any two unrelated humans sharing 99.9% DNA.
Some resort to racial slurs and despicable obscenity.
Because being part of "us" not "them" is a crude yet easy identity to adopt
I dream of the day when in-group and out-group stops, and not just in name.
When we realize what scares us is not that we're different,
What scares us is that we are really the same.
And that is the basis for a whole new game,
That cares not for the differences in gene,
Healing generations of collective trauma and historical pain,
Whether your hands are covered in blood or sparkly clean,
Part of this conversation is yours to claim.

Harmonizing

My gut, it wrenches, at the lies perpetrated
How we buy into our differences just how they're stated
Creating a chasm that is too rarely crossed
That we're not unified is humanity's great loss

Name-calling hurts we label, spew vitriol
No attempts to understand or be convivial
Seen as separate, seen as other
Rather than kin, sisters & brothers

I can see clearly the pain when we deny
Others for their beliefs with no reason why
That we're different is to be expected and it's sacred
I honor your differentness and the choices you're making

Yet in-group and out-group quickly normalize
Perceptions of human worth don't empathize
With those not in your group you fail to realize
Our opportunity is to accept other's truth and humanize

So camp out on extremes with positions polarized
Dig in the trenches, aim at an opponent to neutralize
Resistance breeds resistance, triumph will ostracize
One at the expense of the other who'll soon return despise

If I'm right and you're wrong or vice versa
We will always be opposed a truth that hurts'a
Little more than we can all afford to bear
Collective is our destiny and how we'll all fare

Poles

If today's history is written by the victors
We have failed to learn from our past pictures
Opting to once again play out patterns of oppression
A pendulum that swings in cyclical procession

Solutions? I honor your truth AND don't have to agree
Find power in searching for opposing belief's validity
That requires a commitment to a higher ideal
Where personal preference submits to collective ideals

I choose to value your divine individuality
The bounds of which is the law of reciprocity
Self-determine your life, claim your sovereignty
But infringe on no one else's autonomy

Taken too far beliefs and opinions become dogmatic
Self-expression soon infringes and becomes autocratic
Find balance in loose views held not emphatic
Reconcile differing sides in a dialectic pragmatic

A bit of sacrifice is required if we're to find unity
I'll let go of this for you, if you'll let go of that for me
It'll take work maintaining a semblance of harmony
And we can meet the needs of the most, soon you'll see

Yet taken too far agreement leads to conformity
Our plurality of ideas shrinks and we lose resiliency
Too much uniformity quickly brings fragility
All downsides of pushing for TOO much unity

On a seesaw of either/or thinking let's understand
How we switch from zero-sum outcomes to both/and
We can value being individuals while also feeling united
Harmonizing poles the key to reducing human infighting

IV. Modernity

It seems we have amnesia. We forget
that it wasn't always like this. We're lulled by
our convenience and security, seeming to tacitly
accept all "progress" without truly considering the
trade-offs. We forget that humans are organisms shaped
by our environment. Modern life is full of busy-ness.
For better or worse, our culture is a reflection
of our values. It's all to painfully easy to look
around and see what we worship.

Eight Billion People

8 billion people live on Earth's land.
It's a number so large it's hard to understand.
Just how Homo Sapiens have populated the sphere
How big is 8 billion? Well, let's see… look here:
There's 31,536,000 seconds in a year
8 billion seconds in years would be 253!
8 billion humans with fantasies and dreams
Families and needs
16 billion hands, eyes, and feet
That's a lot of hungry mouths to feed!
Can our resources support us if we did without the greed?
We extract and produce with varying veracity.
Questions abound surrounding Earth's carrying capacity.
There has to be a way that we come into balance
Without producing more as the answer to the challenge.
An average breath takes 5 seconds to breathe
That's 80 billion breaths since the start of this piece
And chart something like 6.4 trillion heartbeats.
It's hard to conceive 3.2 billion. 40% are now asleep
And hundreds of thousands are making love in the sheets
Or maybe just screwing, hundreds of millions in front of TV screens viewing
And just imagine, how many people are peeing and pooping.
There's no disputing our species has done well
How shifting demographics play out only time will tell.
If some countries grow old before they grow wealthy
And whether impoverished masses can be fed and be healthy.
8 billion people with 8 billion minds
Each with so much potential, to put the kind in humankind.

Nightly Walk

It's another normal nightly walk in the north/ the first day of fall/ before the autumn leaves ooze forth/ and as I walk through the neighborhood I have the gall/ to stare through windows into living rooms/ and to my lack of surprise I find tube after tube/ in house after house with families of eyes just glued/ subdued and consumed by the glowing eerie blue/

They look like zombies/ staring idly into the distance calmly/ their big beady eyes absorbing marketers' insistence/ on pushing their services, through all manner of purposeless jingle, squawk, and joke/ and as I walk on block after block I wonder if there's hope/ these precious minutes of life could we devote/ them to something more useful than just the daily soaps?

I see the talking heads on TVs/ some as large as entire walls and I'm bewildered beyond belief/—day after day—receiving their programming, who's being programmed and for what?/ distracted by this entertainment and smut, but for what?/ Just entertainment they say it's harmless and fun/ till our normalization of violence leads to wounded boys picking up a gun/ watching every night because we have to go numb/ otherwise we'd be present with what we abhor/ the pain of our slavery, the system, and more/ so we follow the seasons, skipping show to show/ year after year in front of the glow/

Releasing the stress of the daily routine/ room after room it's that eeryie blue scene/ this is not to demean/ sometimes it's nice to relax in front of the screen/ which now extends to the phone and the tablet/ there's a slippery slope no doubt when casual watching becomes a daily habit/ it's not just the amount but also the topic/ what are you watching? is the content chaotic, erotic, or even neurotic?/ the media we consume can be a dangerous narcotic/ affecting our psychosocial wellbeing/ health flourishes when our media is agreeing/

Blue Truck

They stroll down the street like a tank column in Red Square/ Blue Truck after Blue Truck with arrows darting in the air/ pointing to our future this army's come for the heart/ of our small businesses in name of efficiency and profit/ The ones who can stop it are the witnesses, I mean customers, who click "add to cart"/

This land is prime—prime for invasion, or expansion/ Words paying tribute at the altar of our cult of progress/ this land is prime for exploitation of labor, the savior? He's shooting rockets into space so he can flee when the land's left fallow barren in waste the result of capitalism's pathological race/ but, here's a pittance to save face, who would have thought a website could rape/

It's ironic the name bears the presence of a majestic being/ A forest so massive and mighty it gives air for the whole planets breathing /- the Amazon Jungle - as it's slashed and burned the destruction and construction it's the same function that drives delivery trucks up and down each and every junction agents of consumption/ peddling products for profit we keep buying, we can't stop it/ because maybe one more item will fill this hole in my heart, is that awkward or am I just being honest?

Trust me I ain't no saint/ and every time that box is dropped on the stoop I stoop, down to pick up my shame/ for playing convenience's game, the button says buy now and I am the problem/ and even though I'm antsy and fancy myself the solution, just one more order I tell myself as I add to the confusion/

How long do we have? Two days/ Spoiled by convenience: buy hey! EBITDA and net revenue are up so what can be wrong? The great engine of this economic song and no one has a choice, it's a mandatory sing-along/ they tell us, they're call centers of fulfillment/ but I haven't seen the packages fulfill one's self/ Today's shiny object is tomorrow's junk on the shelf we need help/

Great news! you too can have your own revenue stream!/ watch this masterclass and join our dropship team, it's great/ you'll never have to touch the product as it's shipped across all fifty states become your own boss with listings in this magical marketplace/ but you may have to wait, as your knockoffs are shipped from Indonesia and China/ they're happy to oblige a reminder, that the poor pay a disproportionate price/ for our lavishes, clicks, and floss—their sacrifice isn't in our price, like it's not in Amazon's costs, isn't that nice?

Nature weeps, as she watches us peddle our wares/ mindless consumers who keep kicking the can down the road without a care/ in the end, she'll be holding the bag, filled with the trash of all we once had before it was upgraded, broken, or obsolescenced... it's sad...

Blue Truck after Blue Truck rolls through your town,
excuse me, gotta go, I hear the doorbell now…

Mass Shooting

Shot after shot rings out like a hammer smacking nails in a coffin
Wounded white men attacking innoncents it happens so often
We're desensitized by frontpage headlines and predictable outcries
For legislation that fails every time to hinder this unthinkable crime
We used to be surprised now we barely bat an eye
Do you remember Columbine? The torrent of shock
Two young men 142 abhorrent shots
Fifteen dead students outlined in chalk
News of the tragedy dominated common talk
Now they're so frequent people hardly even balk
As another eyewitness accounts a vicious
Savage whose sickness amounts to another hit list
A tragic death count
Bystanders cower on the ground
As weak men tower with weapons
Firing round after around
Indiscriminately into a crowd
So broken as to even be proud
Amidst the terror and shrieks the silent sound
Of another lifeless body down
In violent rampage
That'll surely make the news
How we give them their stage
So many shootings it's a US-only malaise
So painful what can we do but avert our gaze
And pray today isn't the day
When we go shopping at the mall
Or our children go to school only
To come back on the shoulder of a pall
Disgust rips open our hearts
Here's a list of them all:

Heritage Fort Gibson Osborn n Columbine
Granite Santana Ambler n Pine
Northern Illinois Socastee West Nickel Mines
John McDongh Lewis and Clark Columbia n Red Lake
Campbell County Orange Springwater Trail n Deer Creek
Sparks Berrendo Harrisburg High n Sandy Hook
Kelly Millard South Chardon n Virginia Tech
Oikos Perry Hall Taft Union n SuccessTech
Marysville Pilchuck Madison n Santa Monica
Umpqua Antigo and UC Santa Barbara
Townville Freeman Mattoon Rancho Tehama n Italy
Marshall Forest Santa High Dixon n West-Liberty
Ladd-Peebles Saugus n Wynbrooke Elementary
Noblesville Highlands Ranch n Stoneman Douglas
Austin-East Rigby Bethesda n Frederick Douglass
School of the Future Oxord Mergenthaler n YES Prep
Robb in Uvalde Roxborough n Edmund Burke
McClain Grant Union n Westover Hills
Ingraham Central Visual and now MSU

These are tragedies with at least one killed
And this is just the list of shootings in schools, what a pace...
We'd be here all day if we included churches, malls, clubs, bars, and the workplace
I'm so disgusted I don't even know how to end this piece
God rest their souls, and ours, may we all find peace...

dirty bubbles

trapped in a bubble, life's hermetically sealed/ we live in a vacuum, a digital hologram of what's real/ in summer we go from our air-conditioned house to our air-conditioned work then retrace our steps again never braving the sun/ in winter we move from our heated car to our heated work and back again never feeling the cold air nip at our lungs/ perhaps if we just use enough chlorox wipes and hand sanitizer and rubber gloves and hepa filters and masks and keep our distance we'll keep cooties at bay/ if we trim all the trees and edge the sidewalk and pull the rebellious weeds and interrupt the concrete with a planter that will tame nature's display/ futile actions for control/ when life is anything but neat/ it's messy like my 4th-grade summer room when I discovered video games/ it's germy like the school desks we shared in snot season or you know a pandemic that's hardly contained/ it's disorderly like a cowlick that just can't be tamed/ nature isn't always straight lines and instant gratification/ sometimes it moves at the pace of grass growing as the sun encourages/ uneven full of curves and jagged edges/ boundaries crossed like interspecies border skirmishes/ there's no property lines and measured fences/ and addresses where everything is registered and regimented/ and dirt isn't the bosom of food or sacred soil but the enemy of clean clothes/ an invader to be exposed and eradicated/ clean counters towering over rumba-swept floor/ fingernails long for grime under the creases of skin that can't be brushed off in a single shower/ the immune system longs for a good fight with an invading foreign germ power/ to keep the special white blood cell forces well-trained/ Soul, your inner child, longs to wander lost down invisible paths in mysteries that can only be felt not explained/ time is eager to bust the four padded walls of its calendar cell into dark meanderings even the sun can't tell/ dirty and damp, mossy and moist, wild and feral/ become like tickets to the most popular performance invitations too good to pass up and worth changing schedule for/ Nature bursting vacuum-sealed hermetic living like a child frolicking to the next invisible popping illusion of soapy-bubbled-cleanliness

What a Time to Be Alive

This poem was not written by A.I.
The Day I surrender my talent is regrettable
This ballad of the singularity seems inevitable
That Machine Intelligence will grow in power and popularity
Dreams of rabid robots conquering our world apparently
For our own safety, and lately the rapid relevance of Chat GPT
Is just the tip of the iceberg, it's absurd how much we can't see
If you're a purist like me you're sure it's impossible to replicate
What makes us humanity—our Souls, a very aliveness that can't be duplicated
By code, as if we can know, that evolution itself isn't choosing to ride this wave
Maybe it's using Machine Learning to expand consciousness and it'll be great
Wishing it so isn't soothing the skeptics
Concerned with power dynamics and issues of ethics
We're at the beginning of a whole new book like Genesis
And the evidence suggests our very species is on the precipice
Of a new revolution; will it be dreadful or inspiring?
Either way it contains evolution, a rewiring
Of the Earth brain grappling with paradox
We don't know what we're unraveling
Opening Pandora's box
Will it be friendly? Or a homicidal rival?
Will it usher in the archaic revival?
A reversion to myth, story, and animism
As our means of survival
The machines may be smart,
but can they have passion?
And wisdom?
And will we survive?
Buckle your seatbelts
AI's the Captain.
What a time to be alive!

V. Capital

We certainly are successful.
No other species has so thoroughly
dominated our planet as we have.
Only Capital rivals Language as
humanity's most important invention.

The myth of financial capital
coordinates more human activity
than any other mechanism. For all of the
creation it supports, one has to look
at the world and wonder if this story
has gotten a bit out of hand.

Hedge Fucks

This chump has a wife and kids he's probably even nice except for the work he did makes him a contemptible schmuck these hedge fund fucks pressing their luck statistically at Vegas East also known as the beast our beloved Wall Street sadistically sucking the life out of Main Street with speculation and analytics a relationship best described as parasitic there's greed in the blood, morally weak men gone rabid wealth flows to the investor class while the working man gets shafted by suits believing they have the touch of Midas justifying it all "it's Economic Darwinism at its finest, each to their own ability" a Boys' Club of privilege whose actions drive volatility in markets and at the pump selling out others to get ahead the definition of a chump is a foolish person easily deceived pity the fool who actually believes that using money to make more money creates real value in the world as a worthwhile aim when really it's nothing but smoke and mirror games what's the cost of your trades? short on compassion long on hubris creating material wealth for a few betting on others to fail is ruthless are these actions that serve real, living, breathing life? or are they just useless machinations of a system run amok a lack of imagination from these hedge fund fucks who waste their potential so they can be rich and adolescent in a society where cash is king morality goes unquestioned as far as politicians and institutional investors are concerned keep the campaign contributions flowing and high rate of return inventing brand-new financial instruments to add to the bag of tricks patting yourself on the back for a hard day's work of computer clicks while nurses run IVs they come from the Ivy's while teachers teach the leechers leach while janitors clean suits and ties who believe themselves wise scheme how to make another obscene profit Jesus H. Fucking Christ just stop it! stop buying houses creating a housing crisis while quoting the theories of Ludwig Von Mises stop speculating driving up prices on staples and commodities and arbitrating mergers that reduce competition and create monopolies stop gutting companies like Sears, taking advantage of retail investors' fears, stop engaging in questionable practices that bring financial collapses near, stop buying companies like Radio Shack, Wet Seal, Aeropostale, and Payless, only to announce layoffs while loading the balance sheets with debt Stop, just stop, I know that you can what's it take for you to realize you're harming your fellow man who just need help while you plot how to grow and hoard wealth it just sucks—do better, you'd better, you hedge fucks

Name Your Price

"Name your price,"
The white ancestors demanded
Before simply stealing the land and
Destroying healthy ways of life tribes disbanded
Removed from their home places that were sacred
A flagrant attack on all that was ancient and strange
Replacing reciprocity with a system of economic exchange.

"Name your price,"
The free market inquires
Before paying that wage for decades till you retire
When your hopes dreams potential have little to be inspired
It's the dollars and cents that are most to be desired
In this system of thieves, middlemen, and liars
The price itself is rigged by monetary empires.

"Name your price,"
They request of your hours
Trading your one precious life to work in office towers
In hierarchical structures yielding to blind powers
For purposes not yours until soul's been devoured
No wonder so many of us have grown sour.

"Name your price."
It's the quintessential phrase
That determines worthiness amidst our cultural malaise
Where value's determined by how much someone pays
Ostentatiousness begs conspicuous displays
Of the trendy and chic, and the latest craycraze
Like, hopefully this is just a development stage
And as a species we'll evolve to a more conscientious phase.

"Name your price."
How it drives so many decisions
That would never be made of one's own volition
A collision of intention
Between one's true desires and the tension
Of paying the bills n funding the pension
When all one can mention is the dimension of cost
Like, how much is it? Can I afford it or not?
Society's true north has been sacrificed for naught.

"Name your price."
When I resigned that's what I was told
As if my soul could endure more of it being sold
A life meant for greatness instead being controlled
By the inorganic office true nature never flowed
The brain was optimized but the heart could implode
For knowing but not walking this life's sacred road.

"Name your price."
What does this question entail?
How much of you
and what you hold precious is for sale?

More Or Less

In a world where more is always better, thank God for less!
The two are connected like a seesaw one always begets
The other… or is it vice versa?

More disposable production creates Less care and sustainability
More culture wars turn into Less agreement and compromise
More information creates Less knowledge and clarity
More filters mean Less realistic self images
More distraction becomes Less attention
More masterclasses lead to Less expertise
More money becomes Less value
More talk means Less listening
More doing leads to Less being

Thus the meaning of the cliche "more is not always better "/ everything is connected to its opposite "no free lunch" they say there's always a bet/ easy to make decisions like there's no trade-off but there's always a give get/ what are we giving up in order to get more of? often the choice is easy—"I'm happy to trade time for many experiences"—yet we also lie to ourselves thinking that there's no give or that the give is only money/ when there's always a larger unseen cost it's funny/ how when we choose more of something → we get less of something else/ but when we choose less of something → we get more of something else….

Less striving brings More peace
Less comparison yields More joy
Less rushing means More presence
Less trauma becomes More healing
Less vanity encourages More authenticity
Less consumption breeds More conservation
Less competition produces More cooperation
Less material stuff make More room for living
Less screen time gets traded for More human connection
Less indulgent excess brings More balance and harmony

Sometimes less is more….
What are you choosing less of?

What Really Matters

They dug his lonely grave
The size of an asteroid's impact
To pack his money and prized
Ghostly possessions
Like a mummy he'd save
For the afterlife

She expected his text
This abuse just the next in a long list
Of shameful excuses to work late
Children miss their absent father
A stagnant fragmented marriage
In the name of working harder

Theirs egos triumphant battling and budging
A family rattled, a quarrel never settled
Character accusations and judgment
Relationships never leveled
Holding grudges until it was too late
A brotherhood disheveled

The stresses of a life of little lies
Death by a thousand micro cuts
Of woundedness' complicity
With what others expected of me
If only I'd lived a life
True to my own authenticity

VI. Interlude
And now for something completely diffferent:

If you're really paying attention to the goings-on
it's hard not to find reasons to feel heaviness. In the
face of all that assaults our sensibilities, it is our
ability to be creative, playful, and joyful that
is one of the most powerful medicines
each of us has at our disposal.

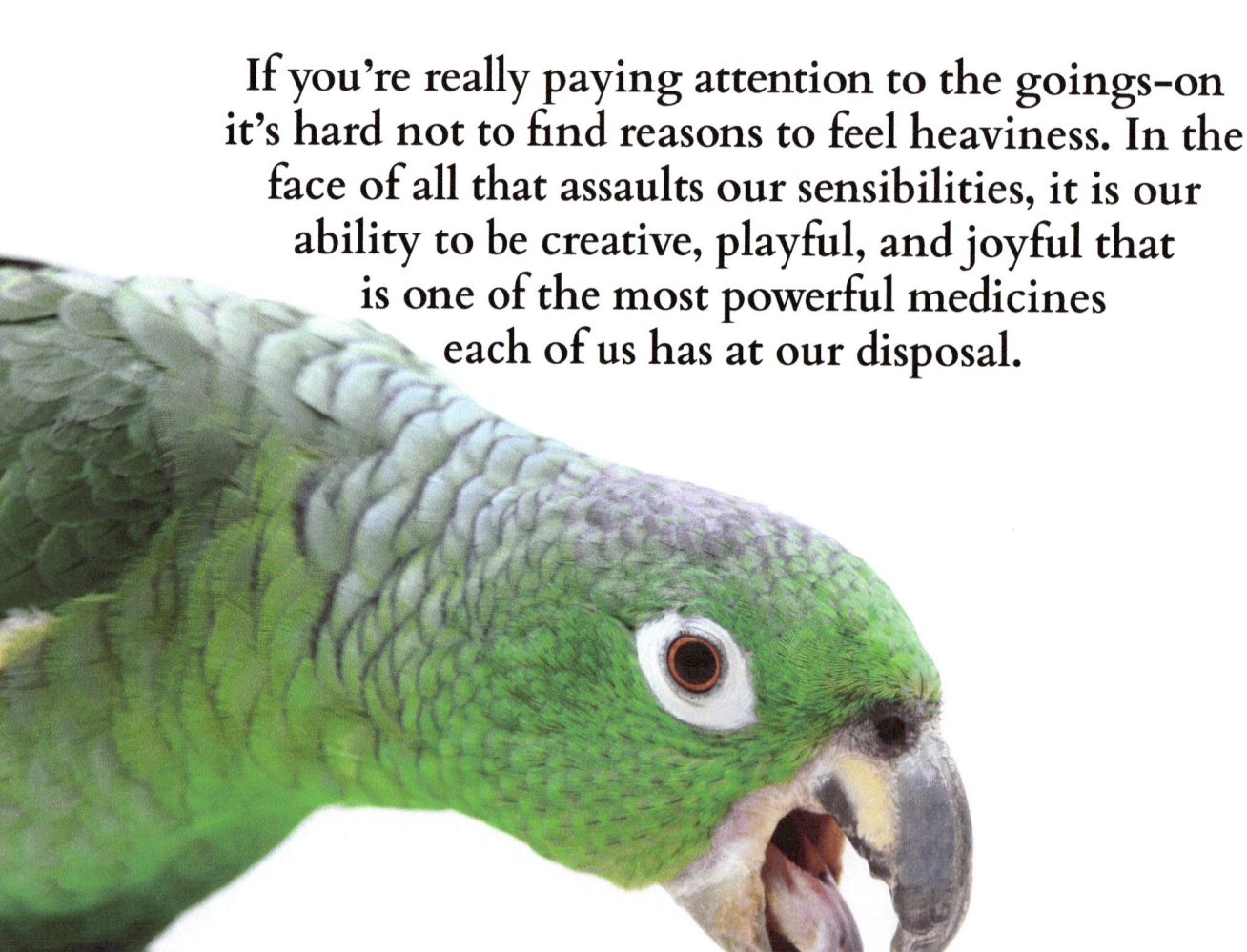

Squish Factor

Have you heard have you heard of the squish?
Known for its absurd magnificence
squish consciousness is oh so delish
if I had just one wish it's to be trapped in a bubble
amidst a squishy squishy cuddle puddle soft pillows
swaddle our necks as we cuddle limbs squeezed as
in puzzle bodies released from all daily struggle

Have you heard
have you heard the squish buzz?
Silky supple blankets
costumes covered in fuzz
completely smothered in love
not lust no snubs it's an all-inclusive club
that gushers in trust its tender is squeeze
deep into sensual surrender
ease into touch the safe
side of consensual it's delectable
multi-dimensional stuff
it's a comfort-and-relax reactor
let's all join hands
to max the Squish Factor

I Used to Beat Dead Horses

I used to beat dead horses
They piled up in my room like dirty clothes
I'd go round and round in the throws
Of a topic in internal debate
Like an infernal washing machine
Trying to agitate a question to death
Considering every angle and possibility until there's nothing left
Except the bloody pulp of an exhausted equine
Analysis paralysis left unchecked in the mind
As if 1,000 more revolutions will help me design
A way out of this newfangled mess.
Thoughts are tangled like a drunk spider's nest.
By no means do lifeless ponies lead to less stress,
I'd have been better off throwing darts at a random guess
Or playing pin the tail, at least I wouldn't be the ass
Who when done mentally masturbating is aghast at the scale
How fast horses weigh up when fixating on every detail
Like a racing jockey trying to train a prize colt
Whipping my brain and nudging thinking's bridle to see how far it'll bolt
Before the Tasmanian devil in my mind finally idles in exhaustive revolt.
The mental spin cycles done, what fun!
The questions thoroughly bred-soaked-and-questioned.

Break Up Surprise

It's not you, it's me / and all our codependency, you see/ Us is affecting my dreams/ This relationship it just brings me to extremes / I can't help but share that truly you've always been there / I appreciate our bond, you're almost too good of a listener, literally, it's like you're always on / Keeping score of everything I've ever said/ I'm sorry, we can't be intimate, not into it, I want you out my bed / And out of my mind, free up my eyes, release my precious time / I take back my energy, it's so bittersweet how you are in all my favorite memories picture perfect pixels since the day we met / And I bought in, I often regret / How I live with you as my addiction, my dirty little secret / So now I lie here wondering what I'll do when we're apart / Will I read a book or find a new hobby to start? Will I miss you? How long will it take 'till I start calling? It's been years, all your applications have been installing / In the chambers of my soul / I claim back my agency, you won't hijack me, I'm the one who's in control / And so we break up again/ And, yes… I would like to be friends/ call this a relationshift, now you're free to roam/ Or better yet, I'll leave you in the drawer all alone/ This love hate "relationship" I have with… my phone

Fertile Words

She left it: the stick of dynamite in the sink expecting the results of a passionate night, my pulse counting each second of the longest three minutes of my life, hearts racing through what ifs faster than lottery dreams, pacing this waiting room wondering what this all means, do we fear or hope? How quickly our lives could be a shaken snow globe so we're here swaddled in a blanket on the floor as I stare into your beautiful blue eyes waiting for two lines like a crowded grocery store, I creep towards the bathroom door, emotions ready to pour like a New Orleans levy gravity heavies knees buckle and try to steady like the personal record of an Olympic lifter, breath is short, door frames my support, is there a stork on the porch? Will I flagellate or celebrate? Maybe we'll abort but like get real, we're two adults at the creational casino spinning life's roulette wheel and maybe this sounds a bit crazy because we just met but lately you've got me feeling great, so a baby we must let fate decide, and I'm sorry if this seems a bit shaky there's a lot of possibility birthing in the canal of my mind, as the phone alarm arrives, courage arises to peek at the fork in each of our lives through the lid of my eyes, what awaits a surprise: is it one or two lines? One means no pregnancy prize, two your stomach will rise, I promise to love it whatever the test implies, a child: none or new? The result?

One, Phew!
(or)
Two, Yahoo!

Human Behavior

There is no drop in a full bucket
If there were just one
There'd only be a drop in the bucket
Why is it full?

If I don't do it somebody else will
Will they though?
If all of us don't do it
Who will?

Let's kick that can down the road
But if we all kick cans
The road forward dissappears
What then?

VII. Healing

Even the most idyllic childhood comes equipped
with ample wounding. Such is it to be human.
Our opportunity, should we accept it, is to
cultivate self-awareness and begin to
peel back the many layers of familial
and cultural programming and
begin to heal our trauma.
No small task for the
brave among us.
A necessary
one for our
Growth.

Savory Gun

Tomorrow I'll wake up feening after dreaming all night of the substance I just released into an old fight I go to find peace with the past I'm not the first of my family to fight addiction though I will be the last with this ancestral affliction that took the life of my grandfather before I was born this nicotine habit it's tragic how its pattern passes its form through epigenetics and marketing it's as insidious as porn plaguing the lungs sweet vape like slushie flavors on tongue I savor your fun yet know the damage that's done when I wrap my lips around the tip of your savory gun like an inhale trigger causing dopamine bigger than the best day of my life it's a delicate dance how we tango entwined a troubled romance no longer anything that can kill me when it becomes an ally I'm stronger but not through sheer luck it takes choice at each craving focused in on one fact this one precious life: my health is everything worth saving

SPACE

The medicine of being alone
Like feeling you're the only one present in a giant empty home
Your mind echoes out sending ripples like a skipped stone
Ask a question the only voice that comes back is your own
Each breath discovering what you really are made of
Uncovering uncomfortable answers like a magic Eight Ball you shake up
A chance to be naked in the mirror minus the armor and makeup
Soft intimate revelations begin to notice
Trembling sensations truths scrolled across pregnant page's locus
Inner protectors attempt to deceive hocus pocus
The longer the silence the greater the focus
Apparently the self is an endless universe-sized cavern
Stillness slices through ego's slippery orbital pattern
Becoming aware that Mind and Spirit are married to the Body like rings around Saturn
Discovering constellations of nebulous thoughts
Failing to serve like a waitress on her day off
For all of us that's hard telescope the soft
Secret self-impressions like the dark side of the Moon
Considering this might be easier with help but no one's coming soon
Just you and the vastness of your own space
Spiral galaxies of fear and doubt circle like a dog in tail's chase
Uncertainty's black hole says you've lost before even starting the race, queue the unraveling
Crushed by the gravity of the stellar distance required of your soul's traveling
Infrared mysteries of your Shadow revealing a dark matter of your own baffling
Voices dressing up as yourself to play pretend
Magnitudes of the inner self as infinite as the multiverse are hard to comprehend
Containing multitudes of the cosmic fabric hemmed
Into us our own unique blend of stardust grown
Amazing what's discovered in the space of being alone

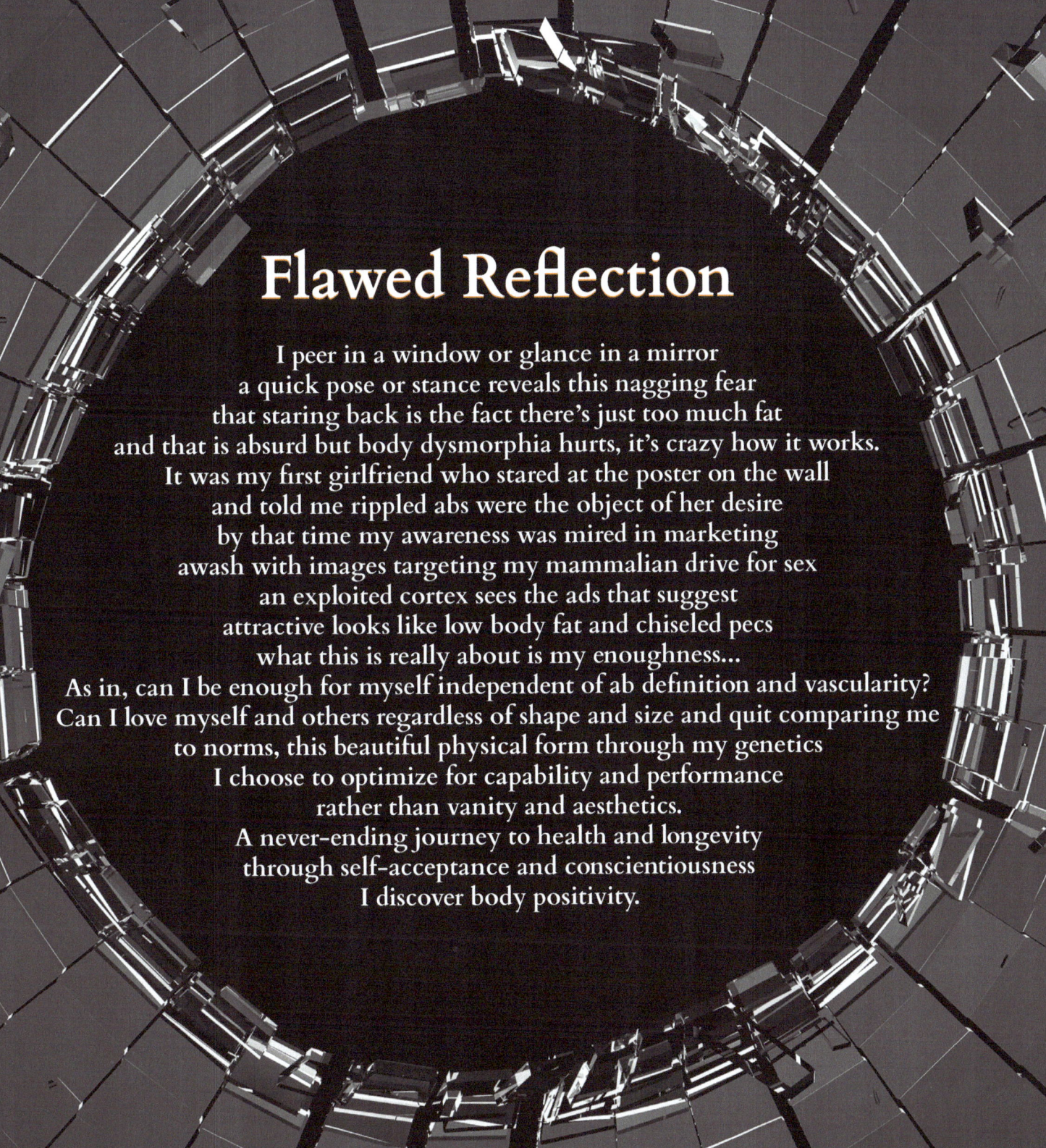

Flawed Reflection

I peer in a window or glance in a mirror
a quick pose or stance reveals this nagging fear
that staring back is the fact there's just too much fat
and that is absurd but body dysmorphia hurts, it's crazy how it works.
It was my first girlfriend who stared at the poster on the wall
and told me rippled abs were the object of her desire
by that time my awareness was mired in marketing
awash with images targeting my mammalian drive for sex
an exploited cortex sees the ads that suggest
attractive looks like low body fat and chiseled pecs
what this is really about is my enoughness…
As in, can I be enough for myself independent of ab definition and vascularity?
Can I love myself and others regardless of shape and size and quit comparing me
to norms, this beautiful physical form through my genetics
I choose to optimize for capability and performance
rather than vanity and aesthetics.
A never-ending journey to health and longevity
through self-acceptance and conscientiousness
I discover body positivity.

Neuro

I stuffed my mouth I had no doubt it would push me when I bought a whole tray of cookies for myself I couldn't show any restraint by the time I was done I could almost faint my heart cringed from the sugar rush I had no one to blame for the binge the only thing much higher than my glucose levels was my shame

I flooded my body with alcohol like the torrential downpours of the Asian monsoon one shot led to the next shot like a western saloon and soon I'm drunk as an elephant trunk at a watering hole how I swam and seeded control to go numb

I pleasured my member with no consideration for how the video was rendered his temper as he entered her warm programmed messages and idealized body forms in all the naughty porn nobody warned how these contexts became a dangerous norm for both women and men self pleasure without discipline we weren't taught to condemn

I crammed my attention with trash talking swearing violent video games and movies tearing each other limb from limb like a young boy with a Barbie doll I hardly thought at all how I was singeing well worn paths deep in my psyche my nightly dose of the vicious and gross the savage and morose images on what I called my favorite shows

It <u>sneaks</u> up on you like mission <u>creep</u> in Iraq first it starts as a limited engagement a little sugar, alcohol, and <u>gore</u> you <u>swore</u> it couldn't hurt then much to your amazement you're in full blown <u>war</u> waged on your neurochemistry and <u>synapses</u> serotonin and dopamine <u>dispatches</u> are hard to <u>stabilize</u> rewiring your brain like a bootleg <u>cable guy</u>

And it's hardly a <u>surprise</u> because profits <u>rely</u> on your most carnal of <u>desires</u> and it's hard to act <u>wiser</u> even if we know <u>better</u> the <u>advertisers</u> use science to get that <u>cheddar</u> and the stresses of life rarely <u>let up</u> it's hard to <u>get up</u> from our <u>seat</u> to <u>defeat</u> these patterns and <u>beliefs</u> when it's natural to want a little <u>relief</u> not realizing our artificial food and media <u>triggers</u> a much <u>bigger</u> release of <u>neurotransmitters</u> then we can even tell this chemical riot is disturbing the <u>peace</u> forces of habit <u>make</u> our <u>menace</u> perhaps the only way down is the <u>titrate</u> like a <u>chemist</u> escapism and addiction are substances that don't <u>mix</u> strategies to survive with minuscule chances of success like lottery <u>picks</u> what do you want more than your thin <u>fix</u> what <u>thick</u> desire <u>conflicts</u> with your lesser habits of <u>action</u> that will shock you into thoughtful response instead of <u>reaction</u> your vision how it <u>towers</u> and despite feeling tired wanting to give up throw in the <u>towel</u> and say tomorrow is the day instead you'll find a hidden reservoir of <u>willpower</u> like a desert <u>oasis</u> a pool of foresight that'll tip <u>stasis</u> you already know <u>how</u>
the best time to plant a tree was 20 years ago
the second best time is <u>now</u>

Manhood

What does it mean to be a man?
Who are the healthy role models?
How can we come to the point
When our boys lead with their hearts
Instead of simply follow?
This recipe born of necessity
Twisting puberty's chemistry
Into self-destructive tendencies
In broken men who endlessly
Assault our nature recklessly
Leaving a legacy of wounds
That entered through the womb
Passed down through epigenetics
Waging war on our women
Through information and kinetics
I just don't get it, how we're living.

We're not taught to see equals
Patriarchy's thoughts we spread,
Puff our chests out with machismo
Abandon hearts to think with heads,
Plural, and often the lower more excitable one
Sowing sexual trauma in women disguised as a little fun, come on!
Wake up, boys and men, inside lives Iron John
Your King in all his essence
It's more than simply age
That signals the end of adolescence.

Contrary to popular opinion
Men do not have total dominion
Over women and land alike
Manhood is not a car note or the bank account looking right,
It's not being a father, or having a mortgage for big shelter
And we'd know this if our culture grew adult men into wise and giving elders.

The path from adolescence is a dangerous one indeed
That requires leaving society in order to be freed
Of the many roles and identities we're told we must endure
They all fall away when we respite in nature
Alone with our soul, through nights of great lament
A boy surrenders control, to move deep down in descent
Into shadow best he don't resist
Peeling off layers of programming
Until he claims his sacred gift
A deep and grounded understanding
Of what he's to bring as service.

Left a boy come back a man
To his soul he can apprentice
His contribution in time will soon be seen as tremendous
If he has the courage to stay strong
Because the easy road of success
Inviting him is the one that most are on.

It is never too late to do the necessary work
Cue a midlife crisis, that's the soul's latent hurt revealed
No more can this deep longing be concealed
In the depths of a man's psyche, his dreams reveal his task
A responsibility not to be taken lightly at all
Before you're on your deathbed it's best to heed this call
Or then you'll look back and wonder
What was this all for, a little plunder, a little pleasure
a great story but how will my life be measured? How will I be remembered?
Did I live a life of service, grow to an elder, steward, and mentor?

And boys, you too are under a great pressure
To fit in, become the mold, and enjoy the simple pleasures
They'll not be difficult to attain
Your fate may be the same as many men if you're not brave
So walk a different path, a journey to what's inside
Everything that you seek is hidden beneath your mind
In the knowing of your soul
That template that you're born with
It is the most important Self to know.

Non Conformists Together

Invincible then, like Superman, our lives indestructible parties, substances, or trouble Could hardly poke a hole in ego's bubble We walked tall through the mall and down the hall chests puffed proud having convinced ourselves we had it all figured out But we were none the wiser Foolish enough to grab the tiger by the tooth But couldn't listen even if the truth blew as loud as an exploding geyser or trumpeting caboose We had no use for the wisdom of our elders No one could help us but ourselves and our selves were in full rebellion little hellions dumping tea into the harbor of conformity barely grasping the enormity Of our longing for true authenticity over complicity with the system and the coming soul suppression You're either with them or against them And common sense was a little too common for our inner critical thinkers Who refused to take the bait hook line and sinker So a drinker or partier we became Taking no responsibility but ready to pour the blame on the lames and unvetted who were finding success but just didn't get it No concern for where our attitude had us headed Vices of self-harm one day regretted A high price debted for our sovereignty Fearful of the very path we were on to mediocrity Conformists chose the philosophy of quiet desperation unconsciously choosing the subjugation of their souls sold to those who control the whole machine a mill meant for making meticulous memes perfect copies of ridiculous dreams hoisted on the flagpole of desire foisted upon the feeble minds failing to find fire feckless feats of obedient buyers guzzling the potion of conformity and we were anything but

so we raged enraged at the late stage we inherited like a dead hoarders home surrounded by throngs of fair-weather friends yet ultimately alone to sort through the piles of influence and programming cramming our attention and jamming the reception of our own precious signal heads on a swivel for a symbol for a sign the tiniest hint of intelligent design hidden in the daily drive round and round the mill goes our lives to the grinder too young to no longer be blind to the folly of mankind too young to be resigned to picket fences perfection and advertisement's designer reflection inclined to rebel so we became non-conformists together the irony of that would only hit us later when bills and children and responsibilities made us traitors to the cause lost in all the lanes but the exit even most of the off-ramps are no-win solutions like Brexit the inevitable march of time makes of us lemmings over the cliff ever the temptation to get out of line for a whiff of that mellifluous gift flowing as if a plot twist a new personal and collective hymn we missed when we were adrift amidst The tempest of paved roads hiding the unbeaten path of possibility whose potential is guiding us to stop abiding and start chiding the cultural chafe that keeps us safe from colliding head on into stories that no longer serve the percolating Glory of our birthright that can no longer be masked there is no ask at this point only the reveal which in and of itself will heal each of our lives an antibody in the larger community a resilience to the old lie's disguise has promised the honest hope in our blood a new immunity
now is the mutiny

VIII. Soul

All of our healing eventually leads us to wholeness.
Essence, our original set of instructions, is waiting
for our healthy self to discover our truth.
This potential lies dormant only to be
awakened by an initiatory process.

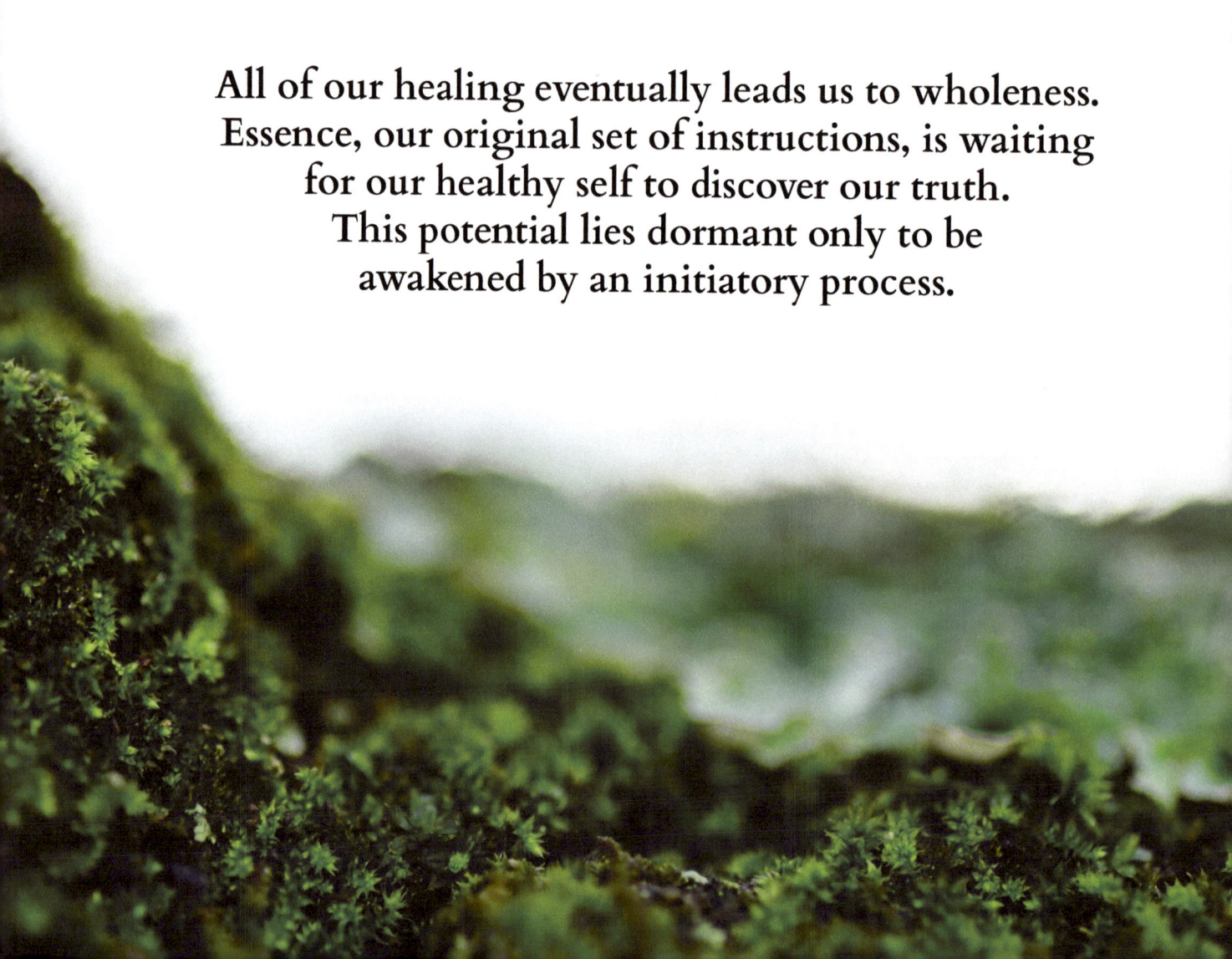

The Puzzler

The puzzler, the puzzle, and the piece
Are bound by Soul before birth
To dance together.

You are the puzzler
Whose very identity becomes
The puzzle as you craft it.

There is a puzzle piece
You've been looking for
Your whole life.

You've searched near and far
Watched and waited
Explored and dabbled

But this piece is not "out there"
But within
And it's been waiting

Patiently calling out:
"Find me, find me"
Its call growing

Slowly at first but then
More audible, until
It demands you find it

Or else risk the mystery
Of never knowing
How this piece in particular

Gives meaning to the many
Other pieces you've collected
And to those you've yet to encounter.

Many of those other pieces
Are worthy in their own right
Of attention, vocation even,

Yet are not the piece
That brings the whole image's
Purpose into view.

You may die
Having never found the piece
A regret, this piece fears most

Despite its calling
And your searching
It is buried beneath

Many layers of programming,
Culture gone awry
Unavoidable childhood trauma

That became your Wounds,
And your personality,
An adolescent heavily vested

In you never finding this piece
For its discovery means
The guarantee of its evolution

To adulthood, thus death and rebirth
Becoming the very image
Of what the puzzle yearns for

Its image to at last be known,
Its potential made Manifest
As you dance, puzzler,

With the pieces,
There could be no other way
But this.

I Was There

I was there, I was there the first time your cave eyes met the magnificent baby blue bands of sky backdrop to the puffy puppets floating on by, I was there when you first fell into the soothing mud, when you scraped your naked knee and saw your own blood, your first fright as the flash of light, lit the pitch night, and your tummy tremored by thunder, for the original movements of natural inspiration wonder, and awe when you would just walk, talk, and imagine, and sprint out the front door to me filled with glee and great passion

I was there, I was there watching through the window, wishing, while you spent more and more time behind four walls more halls of learning, bells and formal formats as the natural burning was buried the teacher yelled a language foreign to the one we learn together before being forced in a standardized cell a new myth spun by education's swift spell, a promise that silenced your urge to rebel, I was there with candle lit, witnessing the starving of your soul how your essence handled it, the brute drudgery as you trudged off death marching, to your daily commute, to flounder under fluorescence, a Faustian deal with the dollar expensive life lessons

I was there, I was there when your nervous system asked you to cast out the blue light of your screen, you first refused but soon took refuge in the blue light of my lover the moon and your sparkling collection of dreams, dirt-filled with millions of microbes foamy frothy sea water caressing the crimson cliffs of dusty desert terrain, an aliveness of fire, a recollection deep in the fiber, of your soul that could not be contained, that defied all your well-educated materialistic civilized linear mechanistic brain could explain

I was there, I was there when you heard, again, my friend, birds brightened your ears, wind caressed your bare chest, pine needles snared your bare waist as sticky sap scintillated your reawakened sense of taste, as the smells of honeysuckle, forest fire, and faint rotting flesh somewhere over the next ridge ground you back down to place

I was there, I was there when you courageously charged into my wilds, a feral hope in your eyes as you denuded dropping the cultural disguise for the mere glimpse of the prize that I hid like a secret compartment in the heart-shaped locket I dreamed you'd find, one day, when the city lights dimmed your attention yielding to the cast of shadows dancing ancient stories on the stage of my old friend Sacred Fire.

I was there, I was there when you laid it all on the altar, when you finally, fully felt everything that's worth living for as miraculously alive breathing life my animate forces now remembered now always seen by those same eager cave eyes that entered my exquisite blessed beauty such a short time ago

I was there, I was there when after years of reconnecting with me, feeling the depths of my grief, amidst my many cycles and ceremonies, it came, my faint whisper of your True Name that shook your whole being like a thousand Krakatoas in an instant everything changed your whole frame of reference became the responsibility to your sacred gift you swore you'd bring forward at any cost

I was there, I was there as you painstakingly resisted persistent seemingly pure innocent invitations of the city lights as they tried to lure you back to sleep yet I never doubted you because I could see deep within you your ecological niche longing to come true

And I'm here, I am here now, us as allies aligned in actualizing the potential of that seed sown in the locket of each sapien lost in modernity while that wild young child inside remembers the mud and thunder and begs: take me in, into that place deep in the woods where giveaway is found and life is good and vitality courses through tree and human veins alike, where seasons sway and subtle days give way to subtler nights, where you finally arrived,
here with me, and everything is all right

DEVELOPMENTAL WHEEL

Nature has the answers to our current situation that too few in our culture have gone through true adult initiation rights remembered only recently in the West living in hearts of the soul centric awakened to the more than human world and they're place in it as eco centric it starts in EARLY CHILDHOOD an INNONCENT IN THE NEST the parents task is the care of innocence youth brings its gift we bask in luminous presents while the child's claiming the mask of ego's form and sense through the right of NAMING proclaiming an identity has hardened attention shifts to nature and family as one becomes the EXPLORER IN THE GARDEN discovering the joy of natural wonders worms under rocks the majesty of furious thunder Asunder towering trees on eternal summer days where the task is to bee curious learning the cultural ways the basic norms of conducting one's self in social spaces then gravity actively shifts from community through PUBERTY become a THESPIAN AT THE OASIS full of fire and Passion and the loins of life felt the task is creating a secure and authentic social self sex is the typical pursuit as is acceptance from the connected peer group here is the root of societal acquiescence too few develop staying in the stage of ARRESTED ADOLESCENCE stuck in stagnation never progressing to the right of CONFIRMATION with identity attuned leaving all societal possessions creating the WANDERER in the COCOON who is now mostly alone to roam having left the adolescent identity behind aka their home all that they've known a distant history center of gravity is descended to the UNDERWORLD below where mystery guides and is revealed the abducted surrenders control they heal and whole and wander the wild till there's an encounter with their SOUL a brush with true essence a deeper appreciation that ended with the right of SOUL INITIATION and all its precious lessons

The Seed

There something lurking in you
An urging its urgent and it wants of you
A certain purpose it wants what's true
What's burning this new version of you
Beneath the surface another person
Longs to come through

.....

This seed, you have seen
In brief moments it seems
These scenes so perfect
Twas as if you yourself were a dream
Your life itself you didn't ask what it means
You simply knew all that's true what's ingrained in your genes

.....

Your true potential, just waiting to sprout
Under layers of programming, expectation, and doubt
Essence can be felt, but not figured out
Presence of a guide can help you find your route
Lessons learned what this one precious life's all about

.....

A descent, into darkness, one's own mystery
Facing past events, the hardest of your history
Embracing the extent of your wounds and misery
Under many moons lament and stay in inquiry
She'll whisper a present, your true name's victory

The Greatest Investment You'll Ever Make

It starts as a murmur in your ear, far off in the distance yet it grows over time louder the call draws near, a sign it's insistence a drumming humming in your brain played into your emptiness rain on the programmed parade you were taught would make you thrilled yet you long to be fulfilled each day running a script going through the motions knowing this isn't it and hoping there's still something more an inkling like an itch between your toes tickling your core that can't quite be scratched on the surface each empty purchase fails to provide purpose each unremarkable day the drumming grows more urgent the more you listen the more you hear your call to service pulling you from your daily desk or enriched register the call reaches fever pitch soul's sneaky messenger is nervous your true emergence unveiled remains unopened the most important letter of your life lost in the mail nervous that if you listen for too long maybe you'll grow numb to the drum's song never discovering the first line of your great tale begging your attention like a puppy's exuberant wagging tail this nagging feeling that keeps catching your attention like a hangnail then one day you can go on no longer, no further, the murmur now the soundtrack to suffering sensations casting off from your life of quiet desperation potential pays no more patience you're plunged into depth's rumbling foundations fetal frustrations humbling as you tremble — now marvelously the semblances of your former identity disassembled a strange new inner landscape gravity itself has been rearranged and there's not soon, true metamorphosis the call your soul needed the drum you heard amidst the absurd distraction you heeded a descent into your personal cocoon where depths run as deep as threads stretched long to the dark Moon casting truth's light on childhood shadow a veil lifted on the invisible battles waging peace's possibility if your healing rattles and shakes loose all of the confusion of what's not the actual you coming to discover the drum's beat your true sound a profound tune a feat of your own epicness ready to be pronounced out loud if there's a way out and there is, it's in, further, courting your wild twin the one of you with a dark sparkling magic murmur in a murky mythic Merlin hidden within your secret closet a forgotten prophet wakens the murmur now a fervor passion hastens action taken on the road of your grand becoming to what wou're made of the shape of who you used to be left as a relic like a cicada your new form a true storm unleashed as expansive as running uninhibited on an endless empty beach the starting line you finally reached and now nothing but your own drummer could sweeten the taste of your true freedom the two most important days of your life being the day you're born and the day you realize your reason the second day now shining as a beacon reverberating as a tuning fork through each new season your task at once tremendous, and effortless, you take tutelage as apprentice to the prospectus of your soul's deep longing the greatest investment you can ever make to yourself — your own belonging

IX. life : nature

This Journey to Soul cannot be found safely
ensconced in the comfort of culture. It is
only by leaving the concrete jungle
for a truly wild place that the
journeyer might find
the first step.
Nature and Soul are
inextricably intertwined.
In the wilderness amidst true silence and
babbling brooks and birdsong and flower scents and
vividly blooming flowers, may the clues to our essence unfold.

do you remember rain?

do you remember
when the first
looming drop
from gloomy skies
were invitations
to stop
and thirst
for play
not for umbrellas
rumbling cries
for us to celebrate
wet skin sensations
cascade
down
around
slippery clavicles
waterfall
necklaces
caressing
all
the magical
crevices
of skin

feet wade
deep
within
blessed
puddled floods
of Genesis
sacred storms beckon
a chance for
our inner
child to dance
under
heaven
lightning
glimmers
thunder
quivers
our bones
like frightening
earthquakes trembling
old fleshy homes
before we were told
that witches melt
which is to say
stay dry

but why?
rescind
an offer
to stare
up and squint
at water
to bare
this supple
body
to the
humble
drizzle
to whistle
Singing in
the Rain
to swinging
and fumbling
in clogged
sewer
drains
an ancient
water logged
instinct
there is no
truer
claim

It Beckons

Out beyond the concrete jungle
Is a forgotten field
Sown long ago
With intentions
Ready to sprout
Under twinkling ancestors
And a mindful eye.

It is only fallowed
By distraction
Of which there is much
For its fertile foundation
Already contains Bounty
Hidden in the lonely caves
Of your deep imagination.

If one were to intend
A visit to these fields
Is both arduous
And effortless
The journeyer themself
A grand blossoming
On such a service road.

Always present
Yet rarely invoked
It begs your attention
To witness
Wind waving through Will
Hope rising on sun slivers
A canvas yet to yearn.

Out beyond the concrete jungle
Is a forgotten field
Invitation to the great nourishment
Shaped as the missing puzzle piece
You already know is there
Waiting
For your lost wandering
To be found again.

We keep nature locked in a cell
Looking through the prison walls
Of our front doors can barely tell
That she's pleading to be let out
An early releasing into our souls
Having been dealt a life sentence
By a jury of modernity's controls.
She longs to be more than just the yard
On our daily walk from the front door to the car.
Keeping her chained under lock, stock, and barrel
A wild beast too dangerous, an attitude so feral
Put her in the hole forgotten in solitary
Dirt and grime, slowed down time, a crime far too scary
Only take small doses of her like a treat in the commissary.
Everyday she cries her appeals
Through chirping birds and dancing grass
Swinging trees deer prancing fast
In meadows and sunsets of color,
Why do we keep her locked up?
Maybe Freud was right
What is this conviction
we have with our mother?!

Lock Her Up

River of Our Own Knowing

Far from sight
At the edge of the river
She flows,
The sacred water
Giver of life
For our sons and daughters
Who grow.

Whirls and eddys pass steady
Dancing
But for a moment
Impermanent,
Inviting the ready
To join as a token
Of choice determinant.

Chipping away edges and banks
The continuous rate
As life itself,
No race to win
Just the course to be felt
A lesson for which we give thanks.

Sounds sooth with trickles and plops
Kerplunks and wishing, soft raindrops
Never stop her going,
Within our heart's paces
Search this sacred place
The river of our own knowing.

X. Seasons

Nature is our most reliable and perpetual time keeper.
The Wise Ones kept track of Cycle and Rhythm.
They looked to the heavens and learned,
as the Hermetic Laws suggest, that
everything flows out and in; that
everything has its tides; that
all things rise and fall.
Like Nature, the Seasons of our life
wax and wane like the passage of the moon
marks our transition from one year to the next.

ODE TO FALL

summer as you wane this Love Doesn't Fade
but morphs into praise as leaves float in their ways
from the sunlight you gave on those long hot days
photosynthesis' death in immaculate displays

when that first leaf falls so must the others
like lobsters mating for life crustacean's shell color
into stardust explodes dancing red dwarfs in the cones
of my eyes prancing like Dorothy on yellow brick-leaved roads

be careful falling appendages soon you'll make the rainbow jealous
the folly of cameras capturing hues so seductive Mr. Hefner is jealous
a grin in delight how these eyes are worthy of such a magnificent sight
that these ears hear the wind rustle a mellifluous sprite
gently twirling from above to be bagged with sweaty brow, rake, and glove
ever surprised how your seasonal arrival sparks this great love

you've grown all summer into splendid maturation
and give once again in death visual saturation
marking a transition and sparking intuition
ancestral knowledge harvest rituals of the ancient

in the air pungent burning of piles the first fireplace's smiles what a delicious musk
different like the type of seasonal light rotating on sundials another prodigious dusk
where leaf and sky blend on the horizon for miles while we gaze awestruck
at your beauty we keep a picture of you in our mind to cheer ourselves up when things get tough

you too will be gone again laid bare in sacrifice of your precious leaves
my friends do I dare hold on this feeling as you slip into the winter it sleeps
a simpler time it keeps watch healing for all that we grieve
a new day will spring beyond this snow if we just believe

Winter Snow Day

God's frozen tears fall like grains
in an hourglass, white rain says it's an hour past
lighting the fire, lids are fighting tired like algebra class
frigid weather came fast, like a maid just a dusting
wind that moons ago was rustling leaves is now observed gusting
pearly drifts, like a desert's curved dunes early gifts, measured in inches and feet
plow trucks flash up and down the street, as bundled shovelers heap the walk neat
Angels leap, into their shadow and back into the heat, men made of stacked spherical piles
wave their stick arms back and forth singing carols through lyrical smiles
after the first packed ball, starts a flurry of vollied exchange
laughter as bodies fall, and dive beyond throw's range
walls of white blow below tree's limbs of change,
white silhouetted branches
these hymns sung to the forecaster's silly chances
every yard now a painters perfectly pure untouched canvas
disturbed by trails, pressed by whipping tails left by delicate deer dancers
lured by fur-covered squirrely prancers, tracks disappearing as windswept answers
the silence of thousands of endearing flakes, one landing square on the nose there
it melts as a smile makes, its way from ear to ear like a field of corn
the landscape concealed by storm, now a white weighted duvet
tucking is in for Winter's gray hibernation, with family and friends
hot cocoa and sleepy books in our dens, for spring we lay patient

A Single Drop

A drop leaps from the leaf

The final plunge after it Springs from the clouds

A journey that originated moons ago

In the gestational waters of the balmy Mediterranean

It, like all its relatives, has grand stories to tell

If it would stay long enough to burst

Only when that drop has been gathered with great consideration

Does its stories flow to the thirsty

Having now become one with the human water body

It unlocks epics hidden in the ancient codes

Written like invisible ink in the knowing

That soaks awareness like a Summer monsoon

A flash flood of remembering May flower

Unleashed in the crystalline structures

It's been waiting eons to lubricate

If such is the colossal potential in one drop

Imagine what rolls in on the tides of a lone April shower

To those who can hear a single drop

Amidst the deluge

Forest

I was just four weeks old, when my eyes peeped to behold, the forest surrounding my family land,
and I grew to love the trees their conspicuous deciduous continuous mellifluous gifts,
that lift the spirit and soothe the soul, where the nervous system relaxes to lose control.

In the spring from beneath the snow, burst the bracken these ferns with their glow, now I know
spring abides, bringing its buds, the flower of nature's tides, they bloom and soon what resumes
is an exciting boom of life, igniting each species with renewed vigor and sprite.

Spring fades to summer with heat and its thunder, and species so diverse they'll capture your
wonder, from under the floor of leaves and needles, emerges Jack Pulpits, snakes, and beetles,
lillies mushrooms overhead flies eagles, as chipmunks and squirrels circle pines so regal,
maple and oak on full display, as the wind blows the aspen quake shimmer and sway.

One summer in the height of green, the forest held the enthusiasm of two young teens,
who hauled lumber down the route, a treacherous hill so we could build a tree house,
by the river it was covered in shade, a lover of our days enjoying sounds of us
enacting great plays, perhaps you too remember your meandering ways?

Its these same woods where fall's magnificent splendor enters the eyes,
how such colors are rendered I, remember the leaves as they rustle branches laid
bare ly much light 'n harvest in the air, red yellows and oranges displayed with great flare.

And then came the man with his engine and might, and despite their great size
these trees couldnt mount a fight, as they were leveled and cleared cut with sheer,
disregard for the precious life that lived near, twas a great sin, I grieve for all
of my saw-fallen kin, knowing these eyes will never see their sight again.

My anger, my rage, cannot be contained anymore,
rip through my bark sap leaks from my core, I'm gutted
how many years will it take to grow back half as good?
One hundred.

My tears and my cries pale, in comparison to the scale,
of our logging magnified, across the globe continent's
arborcide, and yet too few are equally horrified.

It's one thing to timber and lumber by hand,
another to use machines of destruction to fall entire stands,
and turn around and call it "managing our common lands",
as if nature herself needs the hubris of man's plans.

In winter a blanket of snow covers the land hibernating
below, in the desolation there's something we know, this
ancient land will soon regrow, regenerating the trees 'n water,
for no matter how much hate or ambivalence perpetrates this slaughter,
the true essence of nature's magnificence can't be altered by what's been taken by a logger,
who knows not what he does, I pray we awaken because she needs us to protect our lungs.

XI. Place

Having healed ourself and built a connection with our Soul, we come to understand the importance of Place. Without it, we are no where. It is in the very aliveness of our place, home, that we find our connection to nature and to each other. Place nourishes and welcomes us into our true vocation.

Hear, Here!

What makes here, here? When all I see near on the corner is corporate logos bordering both sides of the street like picket lines begging for your business/ what for? two blocks of gas stations and two pharmacies, two big boxes and two fast food placements foods harming me, manicured pavement but no harmony with the nature of this place/ each face lift witnesses this land's health being erased/ we can't help but seeing profits and cap rates/ if it's a choice between green space or a parking space we ignore the voices of the trees and choose the tax base/ for politicians and developers it's a decision that's clear, jobs equal votes today, how can tomorrow vote for here? If we're products of the land from which we came, then being surrounded by the same multinational retailers is a shame, but this isn't about blame, what matters, is understanding Earth's patterns so they can be reclaimed/ partnering with place, rather than paving over it, is an aim that is great/ essence can be felt, it's how we regenerate/ so ground into the land, can you hear, here? What makes your place unique? Does it speak in your ear, the secrets of its flora and fauna? Feel into the field 'n forest fangled with its forgotten trauma inside, remember the dream of the earth before we silenced it's murmurs and cries/ we protect what we value, is it cement? Or what's alive? We can only go from here, yes lament, may it help you decide

Manistee

The river smacks at the bank applauding the color spectrum
dropped as offerings to the speckled collection plate below

A tempered sun glides above the tree line calling the new
day's frigidity to take flight and go

Each slow motion separation from maple when he the crimson
yellow spouse leaves and she grieves deep in fall's throws

The free buffet of sumptuous varietals closes soon for the
slumberous season and all the dwellers here are in the know

That soon the icy moon moves a wet blanket that soothes the
grounds cyclical thirst for fresh falling snow

West bids our undress bodies laid out as bare branches the less
to which we attach the less the stress of letting go

The lover left in the South her furious fire heated play full hearts
before hibernation not too long ago

Twigs snap food scampers from the oven's sights how many
bucks paid de(e/a)r life for that delicious dough?

Tree Says

One day a man showed up
While I stood and watched
He said this would be his place
A belt for another notch

I tried to say in my own way
The essence of this place
But he never stopped to listen
Giving progress quite the chase

I used to stand by my friends
But one by one they fell
Ground soon became a parking lot
Now I'm the only one round to tell

Great stories of this land
Before bus(i/y)ness and cement
Before here's patterns got so lost
How I weep my loss 'n lament

People come and go
So often in a rush
There's much to learn about this place
If only they'd get in touch...

XII. Body

Places are nested within each other.
A larger whole always contains smaller pieces.
Our most proximate place, the place where
we permanently reside, is the body.
It is in the process of
"coming home to the body"
that we can rediscover
just how amazing it is.
All of the information
and support we need to
successfully navigate
life is available
through our
body.

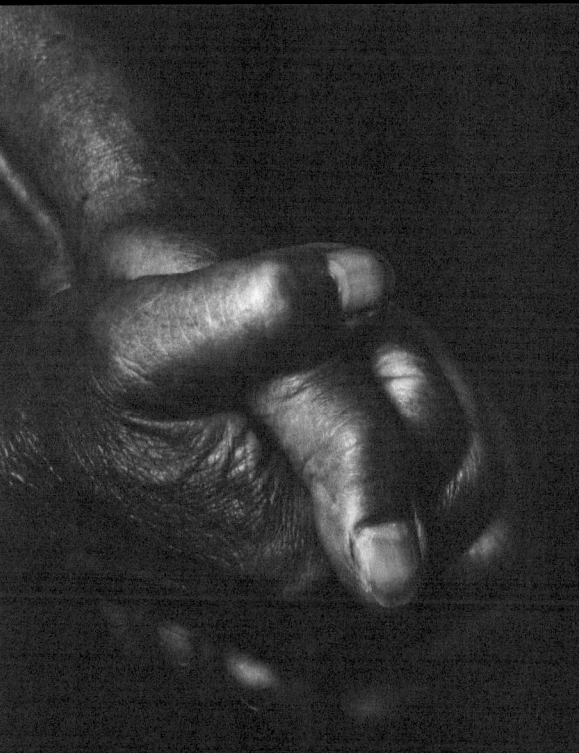

Skin's Memory

Each little scar an entry to my diary
Blemishin' my skin in perfect imperfections
Lifelong reflections staring back in reminder
Of that time when the body was the stenographer
Recording moments in the pages of my dermis
Each mark a flashback to a different purpose
Cuss words enshrined in blood's scars
Become stories for kids on road trips in cars
Much like looking up to tell the stories of stars
Some have no stories yet the body still keeps the score
Like a referee deciding how well you've lived
Badges of honor and excitement
That'll one day rot with my skin, until then
Tattoo the body with new memories again

Your Body Will Save You

My body saved my life the scene was like a dream a beautiful night
at a stunning eco resort after drumming dancers delight in contort
catching grooves like surfers on the seas waves passing below
joyously matching our moves to the rhythm and flow
till we poured with sweat until our dance had nothing left
the group stepped outside to catch our breath
it was in this moment my body saved me from certain death
my hurting legs urging for a seat 30 feet above the jungle floor
perched on the porch's railing feet dangling
when the banister broke body falling back
I instinctively lurched butt bailing forwards towards the loft
using the logs plunging weight to push me off
I came to a squat as the railing dropped
discussion stopped we were all in shock
how had I saved myself with no conscious thought?
I only became distraught when I turned to look
at just how far the fall was I had almost took
would have fell backwards to a concrete split head
my body had plans that didn't involve me dead
an involuntary motion I'll never forget
it happened because moisture had rotted the planks
I spent the rest of the evening stomach knotted in thanks
that's when I learned to give my body more trust
it's wisdom for survival is stunningly robust
it cunningly did what I didn't know it must
have you had this moment? do you know what it is like?

Because I had another riding my bike
the day was January 7th 2020 gathered at the Capitol
were election deniers a plenty
fired up about these liars I rode away fast
came round a corner past an audience of trees
my mind was distraught at our current scandal
in a split second critical distraction
I'm careening toward a barrier momentum the carrier
I leaped over the handles the body's reaction
certainly not mine as I was steeped in political lament
as I flew through the air body oriented
the joint's angles to the approaching cement
a sudden impact to my wrists which survived intact
it was intuition's assist that put my body in the best shape
instead of broken bones from the speed I had barely a scrape
as I laid there to bleed bludgeoned and stunned
amazed yet again how my meat sack had functioned
a feat that I'm glad it instinctively jettisoned
I looked to the wall into which I would have slammed
saw sturdy steel roping I thought God damn
had it not leapt my skeleton'd surely be broken
this piece is a token of my conscious appreciation
the body's deep wisdom is cause for celebration and praise
your body's subconscious will save you
give it gratitude in all of your days

Massage

My finger reads your body like braille
breath scars and birthmarks tell tales
my pulsing palms pressure from the willing
contours of your shorn skin skipping
detours to the highway of vertebrae erupting with feeling
merged with the moment it's more than merely massage that's healing
it's our potent chemistry as I grip your skull and take full control
you slip slow from parts into whole fluid fingers lull
your scalp sensual seminal sensations test stillness's patience
muscular prostrations at the spectacular space between each scapula's flooded faces
a tsunami of facial releases unfolding in waves like origami's creases
the solid arch of your back caves into platonic teases their massiveness
paves the way for tectonic unleashes on the sloped beaches of your gluteus maximus

Taken

The beat drops, my heart throbs, as my sore feet hop, peeps flock,
to the dance floor, bulging bodies twist to transform, the disc jockey's answer,
embodied dancers prance, many manners, styles wet, in trance, sweat,
pulses the brow, a shout rushes out, the spine convulses the soundtrack a debt,
at once paid to the step, stepped right to left, back to fronts made manifest yes!
vertebrate tingle, finger tips mingle, hips splurge and sway,
knees lurch and pray, this jingle frees the soul's sensational ballet,
these head rolls a joyful display, of playful celebration 'n sober ecstasy,
bringing the breath closer to those next to me,
eyes lock chests pop thighs mock flesh talks distant shrinks resistant sinks
start gripping joined swaying heart zipping joints playing sweat dripping
essence vibing sound waves rising,
to the tunes given of ancient timing, Moon rhythms
move us as we groove, peak climbing
into the next drop, under blue luna light,
we stop, to rest, catch our breath, as the night, fades,
it flirts with shades, of sunrise, soaked shirts, and pants, confirm
just how much we love to dance, is evident,
MOVEMENT IS OUR MEDICINE

XIII. Love

Cradled in Place, connected with Soul, having healed ourselves, fallen in love with the more-than-human world, and had the courage to Witness, we come to fully and deeply love ourselves. Our body provides the key to unlocking true emotionality, a balancer for over intellectualizing, and through this can unlock much deeper love and compassion. Then we might just learn to love someone else. As with all natural occurrences, love has it's cycles. Because to love is also to lose.

Ten Tears

I'VE SHED TEARS ACROSS THIS ONE YEAR,
TWO OCEANS, THREE JOURNALS,
IN FOUR DIRECTIONS, FIVE COUNTRIES,
SIX MONTHS, SEVEN DAYS A WEEK,
WITH EIGHT BEST FRIENDS,
ACROSS NINE STATES,
AND AFTER TEN NEW DATES.
ONE DAY I WONT,
BUT OUR LOVE
IS WORTH THE WAIT.

New Love Matrix

Tingley new love abound it's true my thoughts are a merry go round every horse circles back to you **A**nd I can't help but smile as I chipper about my day it's been a while since I've closed my tinder and I just **M**ay all our dates be as delicious as the morsels we've just **T**ried to untangle my stomach it's a rope of butterflies how my heart flutters so naturally we sync no stops pauses or stutters from each other's flower full nectar we gleefully **D**rink from the fountain of what makes us us is so intriguing at the door of depth a lovely mutual greeting meeting has been profound we've searched the town there's few around that'll let guard down with courage to be seen multitudes still to be revealed a Rubik's cube patterns concealed clues left in each other's **D**reams of the future life and how we want to **F**eel into bodies souls divinity **I**s this real? Am I Neo to you my Trinity?

All of That

It happened without me seeing like a gremlin sneaking in my room at night, I fell in Love by accident like falling right, into a puddle it's not something you plan, but then it happens and all you can, do is think is that so? Because that's what love is, it's risky, it's being exposed being naked vulnerable with no clothes, it's taking the risk anyway even though you know, how much it might hurt, you see that new somebody as worth, all of that a defense mechanism pops up maybe a friend or fear, and says Lean back steer clear, because to love is to have something to lose and you know what it's like to grieve why is that a risk you choose, your ,heart flutters in response like a billion monarch butterflies in motion, a flood of emotion rages through the gulches of your soul like flash flood pouring into the ocean, a vast body of your excitement and joy and passion and care, that new found instinct to always be there, holding space and making plans giving Chase and holding hands, gripping tightly knowing it might not last, because while you were making other plans God just laughs, placing each other in our paths a test questioning what have you learned from the past, and what have you yet to grasp from your previous heartaches, will you risk it knowing your heart might break again, and even if there is an end will you move forward knowing that precious moment you spend every little innocuous text you send that brings a smile that each day the delicious fruits of our two energies blend and we continue to learn one another's styles building maps of each other a new cosmos we explore, that the sweet delight of all of that and everything more, increases the odds that one day your knees will tremble as you cry out falling to the floor, calling for help cursing the self that made the decision to go deeper that now your heart melts like a chocolate fondue, even if all of this comes true I'm still in if you're willing cuz I'm really into you I choose all of that will you choose it to?

Flight's Booked

Never get better at goodbye I don't cry at "hi, hello" my eyes look longingly to the sky with The reluctant sigh I feel stuck like velcro it's nice how we're attached securely didn't expect this when we matched on Bumble believe me I said surely we'll have a great time and that'll be that now I fumble, with my words like a middle school dance wasn't looking for serious now I take a second glance rethink my stance on all my plans God laughs I wonder if this is our only chance I haven't tasted all the feminine flavors but baby I seriously savor every minute now you're melting my heart's protection like the Thwaites glacier so I ponder redirection as I saunter off for personal reflection travel means I'm leaving will I return to you or choose grieving yet another loss dammit this love thing is a crazy gambit spinning like a dreidel you couldn't care less about a label reason number 4,223 I'm thankful for the fortuitous force that put our two courses on collision two comets exploding prisms of energy nebula of pure potentialities power now my reality is pulling pedals off a pansy flower I'm begging to explain how we're going to make this work we're so different this is so new how can it hurt this much in such a short time when we're together I relax and trust the grand design apart it's difficult for anyone else to pay rent in my mind I evicted all the others and I'm not even sure I like monogamy but honestly our meeting has the feeling of prophecy how we consciously connect and yet you're moving cautiously protecting your heart from being scarred cuz we're still in the shallow end seeing the depths where there's no lifeguard that'll come to the rescue and I don't want to press you to promise if I go that you'll still feel the same this isn't a game but I can't help wanting to play I'm bouncing back and forth like a pinball when I return will I leave a scar or stay all of this is to say I wasn't expecting my feelings to go this far and I wouldn't have it any other way

XIV. Letting Go

The Buddha said that attachment is the root of all suffering. This lesson can only be fully understood by suffering. Eventually, having loved and lost, having lamented a world far from one's ideal, attachment becomes a personal liability too great to maintain. The most powerful action to take is to simply let go.
Easier said
than done.

Surrender

Surrender, it's easier said than done I know
What it's like to never give up control
Maintaining the illusion of security
As if life can be known with certainty

Surrender, how I struggle to decide my fate
Future can't be eyed though I try to dialate
All I can spy is a million possibilities
None become my life is beyond visibility

Surrender, how much more can I paddle upstream
Battling the supreme for my own little dream
Easier to release into what can't be seen
Finding peace in the riddle of going downstream

Surrender, Autumn leaf gives itself to snow
Morning birds chirp dawns the inevitable flow
Choice is your agency time to get up and go
Balancing vision with the task of letting go

Illusion of Control

If God's laughing while I'm making plans
Then I must be the butt of a cosmic joke
Because regardless how many times my plans change
I don't understand why my vote isn't the only one that matters
Repeating patterns keep stressing
I've yet to learn the lesson of the past
So I hold to my desires clenching with the tightest grasp
As if the outcome requires me fully attached
To the illusion of control
Source chuckles at my confusion
How I struggle with my role
I want a little harder
Of course I can muscle it to go
I pretend as if I don't already know
That my force alone cannot transcend the flow.
Some things are not meant to be and others are to exist
And once I've made my actions it's pointless to resist
Hiding in surrender is a peace that may persist
Beyond the field of ego and furious concentrating
Spirit keeps on waiting for us to get the gist
It takes more than just The Secret
Co-creating dreams that manifest
Every bid for power comes complete
With its very own difficult test
Let go and let God
Unless you prefer stress
And how can you be so sure?
Yours is as good as my guess.
For I am just the boat
Floating atop the sea
Whether calm or troubled waters
I float with tranquility
Occasionally I'll raise the mast
Or drop oar towards a direction
Having learned the destination's
Only partly my selection
Yet victim or powerless I certainly am not
Just recognize that fortune and fate
Correlate with every outcome that I got.

God's Design

I see the wrinkles on my skin as I'm getting older
I see that life is short and it's only getting shorter
Will my life fall to chaos or become order?
My biology commands have a son and daughter
What is this world I'm bringing em into?
Am I overcomplicating this or is it simple?
I'm surrounded by God's design.
What will I make of my time seeds of the divine?
I'm starting to comprehend the cosmic joke
If you think you get it, then you don't...
Seeing clear despite all the smoke
Ashes and ruins of civilization's past hope.
When the ancestors dreamt of the future
Were they actually dreaming of me?
Standing on the shoulders of giants it's little me
Honoring the Sacred Law of Reciprocity.
My whole life, every action is my homily
Sometimes I'm caught between words like an apostrophe.
I'm just self-fulfilling my own prophecy,
May it benefit all our progeny.

XV. Meet the Moment

So how does one meet the moment? The inner work is always the place to start. Now healed, the service-oriented Homo Sapien can take responsibility for their personal actions and begin to consider what their unique role is for the larger wholes in which they are nested. Untangling the "polycrisis" is no easy task. Best to face the hard truths and do the hard work first.

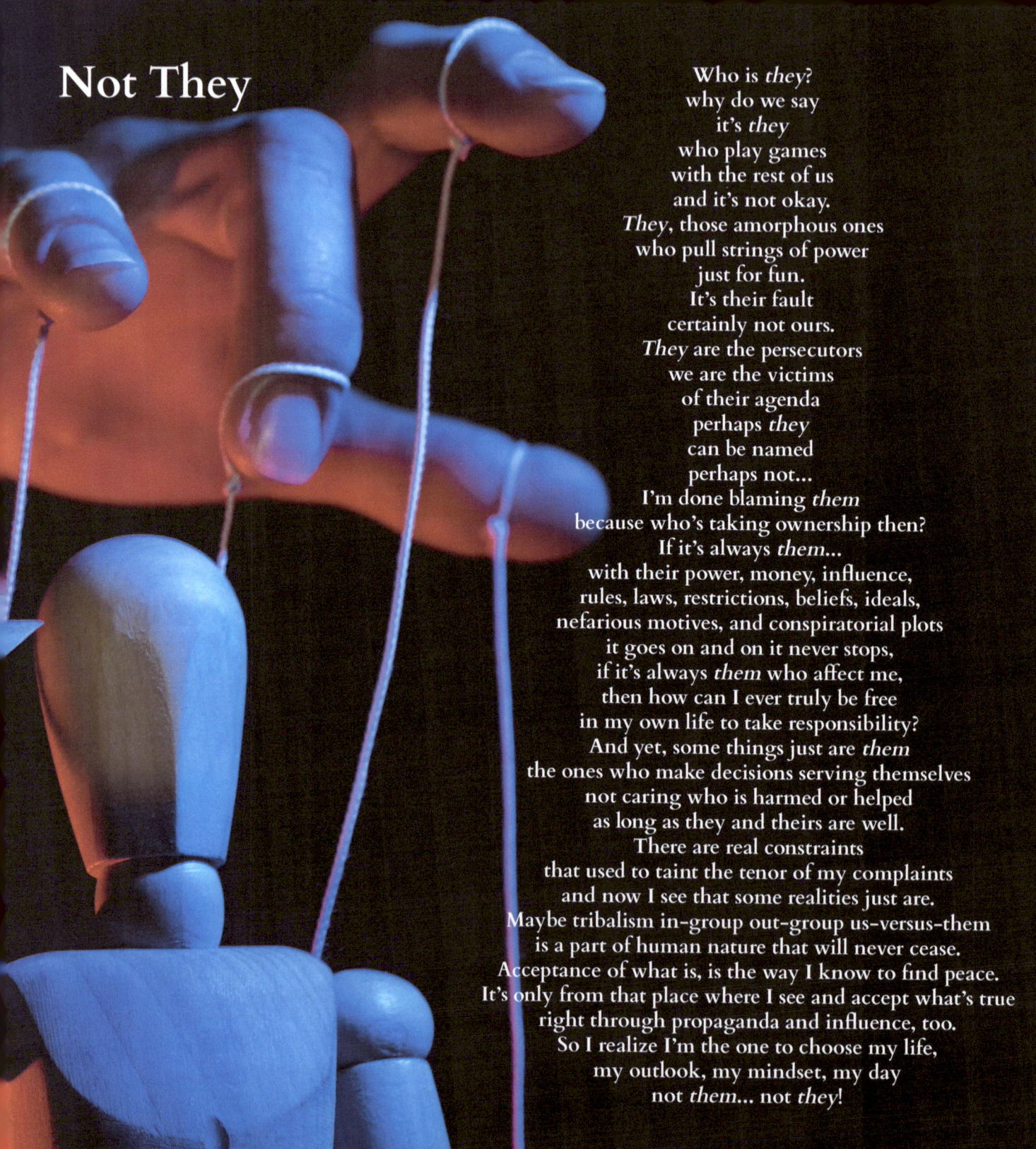

Not They

Who is *they*?
why do we say
it's *they*
who play games
with the rest of us
and it's not okay.
They, those amorphous ones
who pull strings of power
just for fun.
It's their fault
certainly not ours.
They are the persecutors
we are the victims
of their agenda
perhaps *they*
can be named
perhaps not...
I'm done blaming *them*
because who's taking ownership then?
If it's always *them*...
with their power, money, influence,
rules, laws, restrictions, beliefs, ideals,
nefarious motives, and conspiratorial plots
it goes on and on it never stops,
if it's always *them* who affect me,
then how can I ever truly be free
in my own life to take responsibility?
And yet, some things just are *them*
the ones who make decisions serving themselves
not caring who is harmed or helped
as long as they and theirs are well.
There are real constraints
that used to taint the tenor of my complaints
and now I see that some realities just are.
Maybe tribalism in-group out-group us-versus-them
is a part of human nature that will never cease.
Acceptance of what is, is the way I know to find peace.
It's only from that place where I see and accept what's true
right through propaganda and influence, too.
So I realize I'm the one to choose my life,
my outlook, my mindset, my day
not *them*... not *they*!

Gordian Knot

This knot it's gordian metacrisis it is called
solving it's enticing us our species to evolve
we must transcend vices, bias, and fallacy,
seed trust 'n mend the fences, only resilience survives catastrophe.

Top down, bottom up, and middle out – sensible solutions
from energy, health, and education to economics and pollution
shifting problem to potential is an optical illusion
please just check the till, only obstacle to change's
confusion on the clarity of our collective will.

Tend the ground use less oil
mend the town and nurture soil
plant ten trees share the hope
spending currency as votes.

Tell your friends please don't stop
bottom up begins on your block
systemic changes right at the top
is but one spot we put the pressure
we double thread all efforts for
good health and our good measure.

In This Time Sun

In this <u>time sun</u>, when there's always a storm cloud on the <u>horizon</u> hope is the choice of the <u>courageous</u> in the face of <u>outrageous</u> and <u>salacious</u> titles topping news <u>pages</u> Free Will is the weapon of <u>aegis</u> free minds can't be locked in <u>cages</u> forces that be <u>fear it</u> Will combined with the indominable human <u>Spirit</u> speaking truth to power everyone near can <u>hear it</u> make it stick in your head going round like your favorite <u>lyric</u> we need systemic and structural change is <u>hard</u> how <u>far</u> can we delay the <u>inevitable</u> monetary machine making notes not <u>credible</u> printing more dollars during the pandemic than all of history it's <u>incredible</u> incredulous the way we keep pretending everything's <u>fine</u> rather than examining how we discount <u>time</u> waiting to act until the most dramatic <u>sign</u> short-term thinking a bias built into the brain of <u>humankind</u> the hubris of holistic thinking beholding the whole system as if we are <u>divine</u> maybe just maybe there's nothing <u>wrong</u> like all of this everything we made up is just evolution's grand <u>song</u> a <u>melody</u> of intricate <u>complexity</u> flowing from the <u>implicate</u> fractal <u>recipe</u> <u>explicated</u> the Big <u>Why</u> an answer too <u>complicated</u> for our feeble <u>minds</u> to <u>grasp</u> so we dream of the future or look longingly to the <u>past</u> struck by the impermanence of how it all doesn't <u>last</u> tempting to think we're going nowhere <u>fast</u> like maybe we were God's first <u>draft</u> that'd been crumpled up and tossed in the <u>trash</u> with a <u>laugh</u> but maybe Creator was a little <u>past</u> <u>blasted</u> that day <u>smashed</u> on creation, the All missed the <u>trash</u> we fell to the <u>floor</u> what's <u>more</u> maybe <u>Source</u> took a second look, saw the <u>cosmic joke</u> and decided surely there's always <u>hope</u> so now we scurry like ants on our <u>Earth Hill</u> cycles of time repeating round we go like a <u>gerbil</u> in this <u>time son</u>, there's always hope on the <u>horizon</u>...

Eco Anxiety

Rain gales for seven days someone should hail Noah drains gurgle levees break check the forecast at NOAA these four walls close in on my brain constricting fast like a boa this house my raft carried by her tears will they lower or flood all that's verdant and green warmer doesn't just mean heat waves and fire we're past the point of urgent. Warming means greater extremes and while dire daily predictions and conclusions are inaccurate the trends are clear in the aggregate that there is plenty of reason to be passionate though collective actions are currently inadequate. Armies of changemakers we call them Shambala Warriors metabolizing systems from the inside out ones who carry the torch of this noble work with patience despite cause for fear and doubt we're working for the Seven Generations serving life's vitality is what this is all about.
When you look out through the window do you see the coming drought?
Or regenerated soil full of sprouts? Either way we are
the sum of our actions and sins
the only way out is in

XVI. Hope

In the face of plenty of evidence suggesting hope
is unreasonable, choosing it is exactly what is
required. Hope is the most courageous choice
we can make. It silmultaneously fuels our
internal fires and opens up
our imaginal potential to
possibilities we would
not otherwise see.

Hope For Democracy

this is the first time in a while I felt hope, last week democracy was respected
we didn't contest the vote, we let the winners win and the losers lose
all around the country we supported a woman's right to choose
it's great! how the results uphold separation of church and state
a hopeful sign while social media behemoths are on the decline
now I'm wondering is this the time when division and hatred
become a cop fading into the distance of the rear view mirror?
when culture removes the lens of bigotry to start seeing clearer?
the future depends on our unity realizing that what scares us
and drives us insane, isn't that we're different, it's that were the same.
we've the same desires which could drive us to compete like the last 4,000 years
or we could be inspired to collaborate – a feat that once looked farther than near
but today it's a little less foolish to believe that the one with the biggest gun wins
let's all give a little, especially to them…those others we despise
for success is on the other side of the malice in your eyes
so whether you believe in a palace in the sky
or that we become worm salad where we lie
take hope there's ever more reason to try
to appreciate the full spectrum of ideas
loosen the tight grasp of your beliefs
and see what is revealed

Problem to Potential

Some days you choose hope
because nothing else makes sense.
You know being for something
is better than being against.
If what you resist persists
what you accept transforms.
Help us wrestle with wicked problems
the ones without easy answers.
Better yet, shift my seeing
of problems to latent potential.
The pearls of possibility patiently
pleading to be plucked will purify.
Reveal what I can't see
like a book of magic eye.
Unlock my imagination
into the field of quantum possibility.
Grant me the ability to harness hope
and transmute it to action.
Help me to realize my capability
and match it with my passion.

zero to ONE

I win, you lose
I live, your done
Your fate, I chose
Game's Zero Sum

Good for me, and mine
Bad for you, and yours
We fail to align
Falling into wars

Only game we've known
Locked in this dynamic
We're going it alone
For both it's traumatic

Change what we're playing
Introduce a new frame
New behavior displaying
Welcome to the Infinite Game

No longer Us vs Them
Now that we're a We
Turns out we'll all win
Working consciously

Connected, parts 'a whole
Winning can't be all-or-none
Cede a little control
Moving from Zero to One

XVII. Epilogue

Our work is internal first. It is at the level of being that we must first evolve if our external doing is to change. For an ailing culture, art and aesthetics will influence hearts and minds more effectively than policy or coercion. Perhaps the hardest tasks are to observe ourselves in the mirror and make sacrifices when necessity does not demand we do so.

As we charge off into our technological future, it is the stories living around sacred fires, meals shared in community, land regenerated to place-based health, and the balancing of our relationships that will foster the path to the wholeness so many of us feel.

Creator, grant us the courage to do what is hard,
the strength to make that easy,
and the insight to know where to start.

XVIII. About the Author

As a poet, Evan is an essentially joyous man with an inescapable proclivity for witnessing what is often hard and difficult about modernity. This juxtaposition shows in his body of poetry which spans a vast array of topics ranging from economics to love and nature as well as a variety of styles from haiku to verbose prose. As a collection of poetry, Meeting the Moment is an invitation to consider the challenges of our world and the journey we might go on in response. His poetic courtship of paradox, the apparent contrast between the depravity of our world and all that is good, true, and beautiful, says everything about who Evan is as an author, poet, entreprenuer, son, friend, and human.

This poetry collection, titled Meeting the Moment, is a companion to Evan's upcoming non-fiction book *How to Meet the Moment: A Guide to Precarious Times*. The two works together narrate a developmental journey of Evan's own life towards maturation and true adulthood. Meeting the Moment is the process of taking a hard, honest look at the state of our world in polycrisis and building the internal developmental skills required for us to be able to do more than nothing about these uncomfortable realities. It the process by which we face doom and destruction headon while silmultaneously being ever more deeply connected to all that is life-affirming and worthy in both humanity and nature.

XIX. Photo Credits

"Candle" by webandi from pixabay
"Fresh Rose with Water" by anastassiyavinogradova
"Buddha Statue" by Pakorn Thanakiat
"Peacock" by brebcaphotots
"Black Sand Dunes" by Adrien Olichon from Pexels
"Starry Night Sky in the Mountains" by jameswheeler from pixabay
"Hourglass on Black" by pixelshot
"DNA Helix" by PublicDomainPictures from pixabay
"Desert" by __Marion from pixabay
"White Dove Flying" by 6689062 from pixabay
"Sperm and egg call" by ThorstenSchmitt from Getty Images
"Silhouette of Man in Front of TV" by Tookapic from Pexels
"Delivery Boxes" by Bet_Noire from Getty Images Pro
"Blood Moon" by Bestgreenscreen from Getty Images
"Handgun" by Kenny Paula from Images by Kenny
"Mud" by MAYBAYBUTTER from Getty Images Signature
"Iceberg and Black" by Andrew Peacock from Getty Images
"Gold Coins and Bars" by Zlataky.cz from Pexels
"US Lincoln Penny" by peterspiro from Getty Images
"The Statue of Justice" tomloel from Getty Images
"Open Coffin" allanswart from Getty Images
"Jellyfish" by carlosbezz from Getty Images Signature
"Dead Horse" Skouatroulio from Getty Images
"Rose Which Breaks Up" by EW_photo from Getty Images
"Mobile Phone Keypad" by marchia from Getty Images
"Positive Pregnancy Test" by MJ Breiva Photo from Getty Images
"Water Bucket" by Keelia Leigh Photography from Getty Images
"Red Onion Slice" by Billion Photos
"Black Background Vape" by RLobo_fotografia from Getty Images
"Starry Sky" by Jeremy Müller from Pexels
"Shattered Glass" by arsgera
"Neurons" by selvanegra from Getty Images
"Cave" by alexey_ds from Getty Images Signature
"Snow Covered Mountains" by eberhard grossgasteiger from Pexels
"Yin Yang" by aluxum from Getty Images Signature
"Tiger" by peerajit from Getty Images

"Puzzle Piece" by mikdam from Getty Images
"Phoenix Like Cloud Over Ocatillo" by Kelly vanDellen
"Saguaro Cactus" by Dantesattic from Getty Images Signature
"Background Honeycomb" by icon0.com
"Acorns on black background" by Johnrob fro Getty Images
"Abstract Fractal" by Natalya_Yudina from Getty Images
"Raindrop Splash" by Fullervision Photography from Getty Images
"Mushrooms Black" by J. C. P. Ceballos from Getty Images
"Inside and Outside" by Alessandro Cristiano from Getty Images
"Manistee River" by Evan Carr
"Autumn Leaves" by Lisa Fotios from Pexels
"Snow Crystals" by sam_eder from Getty Images
"Icicle" by moritz320 from pixabay
"Lightning Storm in Arizona" by WKIDESIGN from pixabay
"Sunlit Forest Full of Pine Tree" by Walkerssk by pixabay
"Brand New trip Mall" by kevinjeon00 from Getty Images Signature
"Leaf in Water" by Santiage from Getty Images
"Green Trees Near the Road" by Mel Casipit from Pexels
"Battle Scarred" by Jacob McBride Photography from Getty Images
"Night jungle" by Vizerskaya from Getty Images Signature
"Worn antique bike" by Hemera Technologies from Photo Images
"Topless Woman Having a Massage" by A. Tarazevich from Pexels
"Dancing Feet" by deepbue4you from Getty Images Signature
"Wild beach" by Maksim Zolotarev from Getty Images
"Anatomy of Human Heart" by tussik13 from Getty Images
"Heart Matrix" by ismagilov from Getty Images
"Strawberry" by Billion Photos
"Airplane Cross Night Time" by Juhasz Imre from Pexels
"Black Wolf" by Waitandshoot from Getty Images
"Tranquil Ocean" by apsimo1 from Getty Images Signature
"Honey Bee" by przemyslawiciak
"Hand Controlling Puppet" by SvetaZi from Getty Image
"Knot" by Jeffery Sinnock from Getty Images
"Solar Eclipse" by Buddy_Nath from pixabay
"Houses Completely Flooded" by Roschetzkyl from Getty Images
"Pyrite Calcite" by sam_eder from Ge

www.ingramcontent.com/pod-product-compliance
Lightning Source LLC
Chambersburg PA
CBHW042024150426
43198CB00002B/56